WHY IS
FEMINISM
SO HARD
TO RESIST?

IN COMMEMORATION OF THE 150TH ANNIVERSARY
OF THE FIRST WOMEN'S RIGHTS CONFERENCE

BY PAUL R. HARRIS

• REPRISTINATION PRESS •

For all the faithful guardians of femininity—
especially my mother Sharon, my wife Cheryl,
and my daughters Rebekah and Sara.

Second Edition: March 2011

Repristination Press
P.O. BOX 173
Bynum, Texas 76631

www.repristinationpress.com

ISBN-10: 1-891469-47-9
ISBN-13: 978-1891469473

TABLE OF CONTENTS

FOREWORD

How wonderful is the difference between man and woman, male and female, masculine and feminine! It is the engine that has driven many a poet, the joy that has caused many a composer to burst forth in melody, the spice that is so very necessary for life! It has been observed that "there is a masculine-feminine polarity in which all things participate."[1] The best poems, novels, songs, and movies celebrate or explore this gender polarity. But something is trying to 'short-circuit' this polarity. If our world suddenly lost its magnetic polarity, it would be catastrophic, and so would a loss of the male-female polarity of our society.

What sort of calamities might we expect? According to Amaury de Riencourt's warning of 1974, deliberately upsetting the delicate balance of male and female factors would be, "a social and cultural death wish and the end of the civilization that endorses it."[2] Originally writing in 1973, George Gilder said a "solidaristic group of male killers" would be created if society succeeded in eradicating the women in men.[3] In 1976, popular writer Elisabeth Elliot warned about the need to maintain the God-given sexual polarity when she said, "I don't want anybody treating me as a 'person' rather than as a woman. Our sexual differences are the terms of our life, and to obscure them in any way is to weaken the very fabric of life itself."[4]

But to really see how greatly society will deteriorate if our male-female polarity is lost, one has only to consider the fact that when the Equal Rights Amendment was being considered in the 1970s, the U.S. Senate rejected amendments that would have banned women from the draft and from combat. It also specifically rejected such things as protection of a woman's child support payments and separate bathrooms and locker rooms for boys and girls. As everything spins out of control when magnetic polarity is lost, so it is when gender polarity is lost.

All of the warnings cited above came from the 1970s (as did the radical Equal Rights Amendment), yet the drive to short-circuit the sexual polarity has continued unabated and even sped up over the past 20 years. This happened while people proclaimed that the important biologically-based differences between the sexes make the rest of feminism fall apart,[5] while many people predicted that a generation of women who refuse to have babies and who do not take care of the ones they do have will be swept away in 20 years by the children of non-feminist women,[6] and while the National Organization of Women never succeeded in recruiting more than one tenth of one percent of the women in the United States.[7] Why does feminism continue to march on today? The proclamations and observations made about its innate weaknesses and its inability to build a formidable organization are true, and yet feminism brought about more change for women in the 1980s than they experienced from 1945 to 1980, and almost as much as they did between 1890 and 1980![8]

Why has feminism been so successful? The better question to ask is, "why *is* feminism so successful?" Feminism not only rolls on to this day, smashing the divinely-ordained polarity between the sexes, it carries the day. This fact was recognized already in 1986. American culture rejected feminist politics and lesbian posturing 'hands down,' but it "absorbed the underlying ideology like a sponge."[9] The reason the number of feminists is declining is not because there are less of them; they are just becoming harder to identify because their world view merged so thoroughly with mainstream society. "The philosophy is almost unidentifiable as **feminist**, for it is virtually indistinguishable from **mainstream**."[10] This can be seen from the experience of an author hired to traverse Canada and the northern United States to find out why women under age 30 had seemingly abandoned feminism, hated the label, and did not read its classic statements. The author reported, "The women I interviewed had neither adopted nor rejected feminism. Rather, it had seeped into their minds like intravenous saline into the arm of an unconscious patient. **They were feminists without knowing it.**"[11]

Even in the Church, the assumptions of feminism have become mainstream, conventional wisdom. For example, feminism assumes that patriarchy is an evil invention of men; that the Church is not inclusive; that women have been mistreated by the Church historically; and that anyone who says women cannot be anything they want to be hates women. These feminist assumptions have become undisputed 'facts' with most Christians, male and female. Therefore, pastors feel constrained to apologize for historic church practices such as male-only acolytes and lectors. Based on feminist assumptions, denominational convention resolutions are driven to resolve that the place of "women in the Church" is a problem that needs to be addressed by special commissions, programs, and studies, despite the fact that, as anyone can see, there have always been more women in church than men and that those women have been more involved than laymen. The commissions, programs, study groups become "consciousness-raising" groups which will foment only greater dissatisfaction among the women in the Church.

Churches, either by design (in liberal churches) or by default (in conservative ones), gave up the theological "high ground"; they allowed themselves to be placed in the position of apologizing for, or making excuses for, the divinely-ordained polarity of the human race. They are driven to defend reality—to defend the empirically obvious. They are put in the position of defending what no one for almost 5,000 years considered in need of a defense, a situation analogous to being required to defend the necessity of plus and minus to magnetic polarity.

How did this come about? How did what was so simple, so obvious, and so beautiful at creation become so twisted? How did we get from "male and female He created them" to "your desire shall be for your husband, and he shall rule over you?" In between Genesis 1:27 and 3:16 comes the Fall recorded in 3:1–7. Satan slithered into paradise—in between God and mankind, in between man and woman—and he is still there to this day. He is an enemy of God and all that is His: His Church, His people, His created order—including the masculine-feminine polarity.

In I Corinthians 11:3, God reveals His order to us: "But I want you to understand that Christ is the head of every man, and the man is the head of the woman, and God is the head of Christ." God intends to provide for His creation through this order. Satan intends to bring all creation down by working the reverse of God's order; he attacks the woman to get to the man to get to the Christ to get to God the Father: he seeks to bring down the Father!

Those of us who have grown up in Christian homes in a land heavily influenced by Christianity think "God as Father" is a natural understanding of God, but the opposite is the case. It is not natural for fallen human beings to conceive of "God as Father," "God as Servant" (i.e., the Suffering Servant of Isaiah), or "God as Man" (i.e., the Christ). On the contrary, it is natural for man to think of God as 'ogre', not father; as tyrant, not servant; as infinitely out of touch with man, not as man; as mother, not father; and as feminine, not masculine. In the Old Testament, only God's Church worshipped God the Father. Moses proclaimed a masculine, demanding, self-denying religion. Paganism knew as many female gods as they did male, and their worship was soft, permissive, and self-indulgent, reveling in food, drink and sex.[12]

The early Church fought this same battle against fallen man's natural inclination towards a female deity. Will Durant observed this truth, writing, "The desire to return to the mother is stronger than the impulse to depend upon the father; it is the mother's name that comes spontaneously to the lips in great joy or distress; therefore men as well as women found comfort and refuge in Isis and Cyble [Female deities of the 1st century A.D.]."[13] The author notes from personal experience of ten years in the Army that he has never has he seen a soldier with a tattoo saying "Dad" or "Father," but he has seen "Mom" and "Mother" stenciled on the burliest of GI's. If you think they mean it jokingly, try implying that!

Satan's goal is to take glory away from the true God by bringing the creation down to the depths to which he has fallen. To do this, he must silence the Word which proclaims God as Father, not mother; God as Man (Christ), not woman (witches, mediums, psychics). Satan must silence men, the God-ordained proclaimers in the home (fathers) and in the Church (pastors). Satan uses women to influence men, not because women are evil vixens, but because men have a hard time resisting temptation when it come their way in feminine form.

This may sound shocking, but it is the consistent teaching of church history. Tertullian, a church father of the second century, said to women, "[Y]ou are she who enticed the one whom the devil would not approach."[14] Martin Luther said in his lectures on Genesis, "If you reflect on the history of nations, you will find that even the greatest kingdoms have been destroyed because of women."[15]

You can easily see how these statements can be (and have been) misused by feminists inside and outside of the Church. But it can be shown that neither Tertullian nor Luther were misogynists, and neither thought that women were demonic; what they *did* think was that men were predisposed to be weak towards women. No misogynist could write what Tertullian did of women: "Handmaids of the living God, my fellow-slaves and my sisters...I dare to speak with you indeed in affection..."[16] It is the same with Luther. In a sermon for the Sunday after the Ascension, Luther said, "So complete is the perversion of all manly virtue and honor in our conduct in this respect that it cannot be surpassed by any other possible degradation of manhood. There remains to us but an atom of good reputation, and that is to be found among the women."[17] Throughout his writings, Luther saw more noble, honorable, and biblical qualities in women than he ever did in men.

A fragment from the so-called *Lost Writings* of Irenaeus, a second century church father, captures the essence of his teaching on the role of woman in the Fall:

> And if thou say yes that it attacked her as being the weaker of the two, (I reply that), on the contrary, she was the stronger, since she appears to have been the helper of the man in the transgression of the commandment. For she did by herself alone resist the serpent, and it was after holding out for a while and making opposition that she ate of the tree, being circumvented by craft; whereas Adam, making no fight whatever, nor refusal, partook of the fruit handed to him by the woman, which is an indication of the utmost imbecility and effeminacy of mind. And the woman indeed, having been vanquished in the contest by a demon, is deserving of pardon; but Adam shall deserve none, for he was worsted by a woman,—he who, in his own person, had received command from God.[18]

Irenaeus does not emphasize the wickedness of women as much as he does the weakness of men towards women. We find this truth being testified to outside of the Church as well. In *The Brothers Karamazov*, Dostoyevsky has a woman advise a man, "Never trust a woman's tears...I am never for the women in such cases. I am always on the side of the men."[19] Nineteenth century American writer, Mark Twain has Adam saying in *The Diaries of Adam and Eve*, "[I]t is better to live outside of the Garden with her than inside it without her."[20]

Feminists themselves are well aware of the incredible

power a woman can have over a man. One of the recognized "textbooks" of the feminist movement, *The Feminist Papers*, cites several examples. Abigail Adams, writing to another woman on April 17, 1776, says, "It would be bad policy to grant us greater power say they since under all the disadvantages we Labour we have ascendancy over their Hearts."[21]

Judith Sargent Murray wrote in a December 1780 letter to a friend:

> What mighty cause impelled him [Adam] to sacrifice myriads of beings yet unborn, and by one impious act, which he saw would be productive of such fatal effect, entail undistinguished ruin upon a race of beings, which he was yet to produce. Blush, ye vaunters of fortitude; ye boasters of resolution; ye haughty lords of the creation; blush when ye remember, that he was influenced by no other motive than a bare pusillanimous attachment to a woman!...Thus it should see, that all the arts of the grand deceiver (since means adequate to the purpose are, I conceive, invariably pursued) were requisite to mislead our general mother, while the father of mankind forfeited his own, and relinquished the happiness of posterity, merely in compliance with the blandishments of a female.[22]

And perhaps most sagacious of all are the words of Francis Wright from 1829:

> It has already been observed, that women, wherever placed, however high or low in the scale of cultivation, hold the destinies of humankind. Men will ever rise or fall to the level of the other sex; and from causes in their conformation, we find them, however, armed with power or enlightened with knowledge, still held in leading strings even by the least cultivated female.[23]

Feminism is an attack on women as God has created them which, in turn, brings down men in the futile hope of bringing down the Man who is God, Christ Jesus. Feminism is emphatically not an attempt to correct a previous wrong done to women; it is not some sort of 'affirmative action' program for women. Feminism is an attack, a revolt, a revolution. Catholic journalist Donna Steichen has followed the ravages of the feminist rebellion within Catholicism. She advises that "appeasement feeds revolutionary rage and inflates revolutionary arrogance."[24] Most churches—most Christians—have been in an appeasement mode since the '60s. While it is true that massive revolts such as feminism—which is on the scale of Arianism—usually take a long time to work out in the Church, it is also true that mothers and fathers only have a few years with their sons and daughters. We can afford the long view in dealing with feminist domination in church and society, but the needs of our children demand that we take a short view.[25]

This book takes the short view. Feminism is too serious of a threat for to mince words. Therefore the author will be direct—blunt, even. There are four parts: an introductory chapter covering feminism's history, the warnings that have been sounded about it in Christendom, in secular society, and even within feminist circles. The introductory chapter concludes with a look at how far we have already fallen. The body of the book will attempt to answer the question posed in the title: Why is feminism so hard to resist? The answer consists of three theses: Feminism is so hard to resist because it appeals: (1) to the spirit of this age; (2) to the weaknesses of men; and (3) to the feminine *mistake*.

13

Notes:

1 David P. Scaer, *Concordia Theological Quarterly*, 44-1, 1980: p.57.
2 Samuel Bacchiocchi, *Women in the Church*, (Berrien Springs: Biblical Perspectives, 1987) 246.
3 George Gilder, *Men and Marriage*, (Gretna: Pelican Publishing Company, 1986) 183.
4 Elisabeth Elliot, *Let Me Be a Woman*, (Wheaton: Tyndale House Publishers, 1976) 93.
5 David J. Ayers, "The Inevitability of Failure," *Recovering Biblical Manhood and Womanhood*, John Piper and Wayne Grudem, eds., (Wheaton: Crossways Books, 1991) 315.
6 Mary Pride, *The Way Home*, (Westchester: Crossway Books, 1985) 157.
7 George Alan Rekers, "Psychological Foundations for Rearing Masculine Boys and Feminine Girls," in *Recovering Biblical Manhood and Womanhood*, 295.
8 Mary A. Kassian, *The Feminist Gospel*, (Wheaton: Crossway Books, 1992) 238.
9 Gilder, viii.
10 Kassian, 251.
11 Kassian, 252.
12 Ratibor-Ray M. Jurjevich, *The Contemporary Faces of Satan*, (Denver: Ichthys Books, 1985) 258.
13 Will Durant, *Ceasar and Christ*, (New York: MJF Books, 1944) 526-527.
14 Stephen B. Clark, *Man and Woman in Christ*, (Ann Arbor: Servant Books, 1980) 320.
15 Martin Luther, *Luther's Works*, vol. 2, ed. Jaroslav Pelikan, "Lectures on Genesis," trans. Geroge Schick, (St. Louis: Concordia, 1960) 29.
16 Clark, 320.
17 Martin Luther, *Sermons of Martin Luther*, Vol. VII, (Grand Rapids: Baker Book House, 1983) 308.
18 The Ante-Nicene Fathers, eds. Alexander Roberts & James Donaldson, Vol. 1, (Grand Rapids: Eerdmans Publishing, 1987) 571.
19 Fyodor Dostoevsky, *The Brothers Karamazov*, trans. Alexandra Kroptkin, (Garden City: The Literary Guild of America, 1949) 136.
20 Mark Twain, *The Diaries of Adam and Eve*, (New York: American Heritage Press, 1971) 31.
21 *The Feminist Papers*, ed. Alice S. Rossi, (Boston: Northeastern University Press, 1973) 12.
22 Rossi, 24.
23 Rossi, 114-115.
24 Donna Steichen, *Ungodly Rage*, (San Francisco: Ignatius Press, 1991) 372.
25 Steichen, 392.

CHAPTER 1
AN INTRODUCTION TO FEMINISM

In tracing the history of feminism, one could go all the way back to the Garden of Eden and Eve's desire to be as God and to be the spiritual leader in the home. We could then trace the path of feminism through Sarah as she directed Abraham to take her maid in a rational attempt to fulfill God's promise of a son. We could pick it up in Rebekah as well as she made sure her son Jacob got the blessing promised him. We could find feminism in Miriam as she rises up against Moses, inciting Aaron against him, too. We could go on following its trail through Jezebel and her daughter Athaliah hundreds of years later in the Book of Kings. The spirit of feminism passes on into the New Testament, too. It is present when Herodias bedevils Herod with the dancing of her daughter and succeeds in getting the head of God's prophet, John. The feminist spirit is there when James and John's mother seeks the place she desires for her sons. We can find the feminist spirit all the way to the end of the Bible in the Book of Revelation where we meet another Jezebel doing much damage in the Church of Thyatira.

The trail of feminism is an unbroken one that can be followed right down to our day. There have always been men and women, societies and "churches" that rebelled against God's ordering of creation and rejected the male-female polarity. But it was not until the nineteenth century that one can find a recognizable, sustained feminist movement. From the nineteenth century on, feminism (or the 'woman movement' as it was called then) began moving *away* from God. Each generation took a step away from where it plateaued for a while before taking the next step which it always believed was *up* for women but was in reality *away* from God. But these steps away from God in the nineteenth and twentieth century were preceded by a rejection of God in the eighteenth century.

It would be hard to overstate how thoroughly God was rejected in the eighteenth century. That century produced what the world considers to be three of her greatest historians: Voltaire, Hume, and Gibbon. These men were all grounded in philosophy, and all three rejected the supernatural. As a consequence, they interpreted history in non-theological terms.[1] God was left out of the equation. History was no longer *His*-story (that is God's story); some other principle of understanding why things happened the way they did was needed. Eventually, in the nineteenth century, such things as random chance, economic forces, environment, psychology, sociology, and evolution would be used to understand history and the men and women who made it.

But did this non-theological outlook really affect everyday people? Will Durant quotes eighteenth century English statesmen Lord Hervey:

> This fable of Christianity...was now [1728] so exploded in England that any man of fashion or condition would have been almost as much ashamed to own himself a Christian as formerly he would have been to profess himself none. Even the women who prided themselves at all on their understanding took care to let people know that Christian prejudices were what they despised being bound by.[2]

And Alexis de Tocqueville, a famous French writer of the nineteenth century, observed in 1856 that at the end of the eighteenth century all religious belief fell into universal discredit.[3]

With God out of the picture, some other explanation for the created order (including the male-female polarity) needed to be found. Hence evolution was born, and with its birth came the death of objective science. Man could no longer study the world around him objectively because he was no longer master over it but saw himself as a product of it. Once an objective view of the world was lost, a subjective view became normative through the new "science" called psychology. The subjective opinions of social scientists became as the Word of God to many.

This development had a direct role in the rise of feminism as Betty Friedan first laid out in her 1963 work, *The Feminine Mystique*. Freidan, herself trained in Freudian psychology, says, "The feminine mystique [the image to which contemporary society expected women to conform] derived its power from Freudian thought....How can an educated American woman, who is not herself an analyst, presume to question a Freudian truth?"[4] Freidan goes on to say, "After the depression, after the war, Freudian psychology became much more than a science of human behavior, a therapy for suffering. It became an all-embracing American ideology, a new religion."[5]

Through Freudian psychology, the word of man became as the Word of God. Women rebelled against God's Word and insisted that their words, their vision of reality, had just as much claim to divinity as any man's did. In the 1960s, Roman Catholic feminist Mary Daly proclaimed that women would never really be free until they won the right to name themselves, reality, and God. However, Mary Daly was only claiming for women what unbelieving men had been claiming for themselves since the eighteenth century.

But we have gone too far, too fast; let us go back to the nineteenth century. Before doing so, let us look briefly at the term "feminist." This term is used for anyone, male or female, who rejects the God-given roles of male and female in the home, church, or society. Since the close of the nineteenth century, almost all secular literature on the subject recognizes two types of feminism. Although different terms are used, the basic distinction is that one group, usually called 'radical' feminists, seeks to eliminate sex-specific limitations. The other group, usually referred to as just 'feminists', seeks to recognize (rather than quash) qualities and habits called 'female', protect the interests women have already defined as their own, and give women a much greater scope of influence.[6]

This basic distinction is used in the 1994 book, *Who Stole Feminism?*, Christina Hoff Sommers divides feminism into "equity" and "gender" feminists. Equity feminists are those who follow Elizabeth Cady Stanton in the so-called "First Wave" of feminism which began in the mid-nineteenth century. Equity feminists seek equality (not interchangeability) with men. Gender feminists are the so-called "Second Wave" of feminism. Sommers, who identifies herself as an equity feminist, says the Second Wave, while radical and weird, "are articulate, prone to self-dramatization, and chronically offended." The Second Wave, gender feminists are at war with men and want to overthrow their institutions and replace them with their own.[7]

Another author, writing in 1980, divides feminists into "social" and "radical." The social want to help the woman's situation and the radical want to overthrow the man's situation.[8] Writing in the early 1900s, feminist Charlotte Perkins Gilman also distinguished between two types of feminist. Her American brand she called "Human Feminists" and the European (Swedish) brand of Ellen Key's she called "Female Feminists." On the one hand, Human or American feminists, according to Gilman, advocated invading the male domain of economics and politics. The Female or European feminists, on the other hand, advocated the emphasizing of the role of motherhood and sexual freedom.[9]

It is obvious that "equity," "social," and "European" or "Female" feminism all come from one well, and "gender," "radical," and "American" or "Human" feminism come from another well. What is not recognized, especially among

Christians, is that the two types of feminism, while coming from different wells on the surface, share the same aquifer below. The two do not, as many Christian feminists would argue, differ in *kind*; they only differ in *degree*. To accept the assumptions and conclusions of the less radical group is to leave yourself (or your children) vulnerable to the more radical group. It is the way of the Serpent of old to get the wagon leaning a certain direction and then to push in the direction it is leaning. "Equity," "social," or "Female" feminists have gotten the Church leaning the feminist direction. Leaning at the sharp angle it is, the Church is hard pressed to find the footing to push against the "gender," "radical," or "Human" feminists.

Despite the radical rejection of Christianity in the eighteenth century, in America the nineteenth century did not start out in rebellion against the Biblical order of creation; on the contrary, there were many indications that people accepted and lived according to that order. One historian tells us, "The idea of a set or 'suite' of identically styled but gender-distinctive furniture signified the separate but originally related 'spheres' of ideal family life."[10] This same historian testifies concerning nineteenth century America:

> The husband's obligation was to love and cherish his wife, but his behavior was paradoxically linked to her willingness to submit to him cheerfully in all areas of life. For women who wondered why roles could not sometimes be reversed, the standard answer was a tautology: Only a "henpecked" man would accept a role reversal, and the true-spirited woman 'would blush to acknowledge herself the wife of such a dastardly man as would submit to such treatment.'[11]

But we do not have to be content with secondary sources on this matter. French social philosopher Alexis de Tocqueville is a primary source concerning life in nineteenth century America, having written his *Democracy in America* after touring the nation in the 1830s. He testifies to the fact that the women of the nineteenth century knew how to submit to men, the men knew how to sacrifice for and exalt women, and that this system did not demean women:

> As for myself, I do not hesitate to avow that although the women of the United States are confined within the narrow circle of domestic life, and their situation is in some respects one of extreme dependence, I have nowhere seen woman occupying a loftier position; and if I were asked, now that I am drawing to the close of this work, in which I have spoken of so many important things done by the Americans, to what the singular prosperity and growing strength of that people ought mainly to be attributed, I should reply: to the superiority of their women.[12]

Still, something went terribly wrong in the nineteenth century. One indication of this is that after over 1,850 years of almost unanimous testimony against women's ordination, women were ordained. The Universalist Church was the first to ordain women, doing so in 1853. The Congregationalist Church followed that same year. The Wesleyan Methodists did the same sometime in the early 1850s. By the late 1800s the Baptists were doing it. The Pentecostals were next, ordaining women in the early 1900s. Lutherans in Norway did it in 1938; Danish Lutherans followed in 1947, and Swedish Lutherans in 1953. The United Presbyterians did it in 1956. American Lutherans did so in 1970.[13] Since then, the Anglicans and the Episcopalians have ordained women. The Roman Catholic, the Orthodox, and a few small Protestant bodies are the only ones that have maintained the catholic, apostolic faith in this matter.

A second indication that something went terribly wrong at a very basic level, not just with women but with men and society in general in the 1800s, is the catastrophic decline in the fertility rate. From 1800 to 1900 the fertility rate plummeted from 7.04 to 3.56 children per woman, a decline of 3.48 children per woman.[14] From 1900 to 1990 (the time that most people assume the decline occurred), the drop was only one of 1.76 from 3.56 children per woman to 1.8. In order for a population merely to replace itself—not growing at all but merely maintaining present levels—the fertility rate needs to be 2.1 children per woman.

Something happen during this so-called "Age of Innocence"; something happened during Victoria's era. Stephen Clark believes he knows what that "something" was:

> Up until the last century, there has been a continuous teaching about the equality of spiritual status in Christ of man and woman, about the husband being the head of the family, and about the husband and the wife having different spheres of responsibility. Catholics, Orthodox, the major reformers, the Evangelical movement—all were agreed on this point.[15]

Why did this teaching cease in the nineteenth century? Because women themselves started being the authoritative teachers, particularly in spiritual and moral matters. Women became authorities in the nineteenth century, not because of their education, but because of their gender. Much as Rousseau, the French philosopher and social reformer, had put children and the noble savage on pedestals in the eighteenth century because of their innate characteristics which distinguished them from mature, civilized men, so women were put on a pedestal in the nineteenth century simply because they were women. They were regarded as having superior sentiments, morals, virtues, and religion. But who elevated them? Liberal Protestant clergymen, according to feminist Ann Douglas' book, *The Feminization of American Culture.*

How did such a strange turn of events come about? The Church was originally established in the United States, i.e., officially recognized and supported by the government.

This status lasted until 1833 when the last denomination was formally disestablished. As long as the Church was officially established, clergymen held high status in society overall. But when the Church was disestablished, the status of the clergymen fell precipitously; their opinions were no longer sought or valued by government, business or men in general. However, the women still listened to them and sought their advice.

Women in the nineteenth century kept clergymen on the heights of the pedestals they enjoyed. They, in turn, put women in general, and mothers in particular, on a pedestal. Clergymen put forth women as the moral arbiters, the guardians of virtue. Men, for the most part, were regarded as just the opposite: they had no morals or virtues apart from women. Then, as now, many men liked this view because there was no expectation for them to be moral or virtuous.

The domain of women was the home up until this time. The movement to abolish slavery brought them out of their homes and into society. Here was a moral issue that certainly required the moral arbiters of society to speak. Contrary to popular misconceptions, women were never a large part of the Abolition Movement, making up no more than ten to fifteen percent of it.[16] However, because slavery was a political issue, it brought women into the political arena for the first time in America. Through their association with the Abolition Movement, they learned how to organize, the realities of politics, and the power of the vote. Women viewed their involvement in the Abolition Movement as a success, and they believed their voice ought to be heard on other issues confronting society and government. Betty Freidan agrees with this viewpoint saying in her 1963 classic, *The Feminine Mystique*: "The call to the first Woman's Rights convention came about because an educated woman, who had already participated in shaping society as an abolitionist, came face to face with the realities of a housewife's drudgery and insolation in a small town."[17]

But at this stage, the issues that would later come to

define feminism were not raised. The "woman movement" (as it was called) did not champion radical causes. Still, hostility toward men, the Church, and marriage was definitely showing up in literature. These things would have been rejected outright by conventional society at the time, so they could not be publicly championed, but they could be aired and accepted in a fictional framework.[18]

The first women's rights meeting in American history took place July 19 and 20, 1848 in Seneca Falls, New York. Two facts about this conference need to be highlighted which are normally only mentioned in passing: Quaker women were a prominent part of the conference, and the conference was located in upstate New York.

The Quakers are known, among other things, for their belief that God speaks to individuals through the "inner light" and for their encouraging women to be ministers. Several of the leaders of the nineteenth century woman movement either started out in the Quaker religion or converted to it. Already at the end of the eighteenth century, Quakers gave opportunities to women to lead and preach, and they made few role distinctions between the sexes.[19]

The Quakers were involved in several areas which later became definitive ones for feminists. Radical feminist Rosemary Ruether notes that the Quakers were one group, "who touched on the connection between the liberation of the oppressed and the reconciliation of the feminine and the masculine."[20] Modern feminism is strongly connected to both Liberation Theology and to the assumption that feminine and masculine differences should be ignored or overcome through education, training, and/or legislation.

Another thing Quakers are known for is their pacifism. This, too, has been a theme of feminism. When World War I broke out, feminists chained themselves to the fence of the White House in protest against the war and for the right to vote. The majority of these women were Quakers.[21]

Psychology is another issue that is very modern yet is connected to Quakerism. While not exclusively or even primarily a domain of feminism, feminists do draw much of their support from psychology. Also, women make up the majority of those who go to psychologists or therapists, as well as the majority of undergraduates in that field of study. The Quakers of Pennsylvania were the first to establish asylums where the condition of insanity was treated as a disease.[22] (Although it is granted that some types of mental problems are caused by physical diseases of the brain, the assumption that all insanity must be caused by a "disease" has wrought all kinds of folly in modern society.)

The location of the conference is another fact that should be highlighted. Seneca Falls is in upstate New York. It is not only the birthplace of feminism but of Mormonism, too. (This area was also known for being heavily influenced by Quakers.) It was called the "Burned-Over District" because of the frequency of revivals there. It was the seedbed for many early nineteenth century reform groups.[23] Also of note is the fact that the Fox sisters began their table rapping seances in this region in 1848.[24] Here is a present day historian's view of this area:

> An area from Vermont stretching across western New York was the most prolific of prophets, seers, and others with new revelations. 'This was the area,' says an historian of these movements, 'that was sometimes called the "burnt" district because it had been swept by so many fires of religious excitement. Anything new in the way of religious belief seemed attractive to the jaded appetites of its inhabitants and no new sect lacked some following.'[25]

Surely, it is more than coincidence that the feminist movement which has brought us abortion on demand, priestesses, goddess worship, witchcraft in the Church, and many more perversions originated in an area and at a time when Satan was having a heyday. Seemingly bereft at the time of faithful pastors and churches, this area churned out several demon-inspired movements that ignited fires which still burn to this day.

What would become the feminist movement was spawned in upstate New York in 1848, but it went by a different name. "People in the nineteenth century did not say *feminism*. They spoke of the advancement of woman or the cause of woman, woman's rights, and woman suffrage."[26] In fact, it was not until the turn of the century that the words "feminism" and "feminist" no longer required quotation marks in the print media.[27] By 1910, the word "feminism" came into wide usage and another "-ism" was born. "As an *ism* (an ideology) it presupposed a set of principles not necessarily belonging to every woman—nor limited to women."[28] In other words, what was born was not just a new way of looking at women but a new way of looking at the world—a new world view. It would become a new way of looking at God, and in fact already in its neophyte stage it was well on the way to doing just that. Feminist Nancy Cott tells us, "Feminism severed the ties the woman movement [of the nineteenth century] had to Christianity and conventional respectability."[29]

While the woman movement was changing from movement to "-ism," the cause was carried on. It took 72 years (1848–1920) and two generations of women to win the right to vote. The five volume *History of Woman Suffrage*, published in 1882, calls this drive, "a rebellion such as the world had never before seen."[30] This is true in more ways than one: It was not only a rebellion against the established order and God's order, it was a rebellion against women. Carl Degler makes this clear in his book, *At Odds*: "[E]ven on the eve of the acceptance of suffrage, it was hard to make a case for a compelling interest among women in achieving the vote."[31] In 1895 the Massachusetts legislature permitted women to vote with men to settle the suffrage issue. There were 187,000 votes against suffrage and 110,000 for it. But the interesting thing is that while 87,000 men voted for the change only 23,000 women did![32] Writing in 1890, a woman suffragist said, "'The women don't want the vote' is the 'stunner' that we friends of the cause have to meet at every hand..."[33] The same phenomenon can be seen in the case of the Equal Rights Amendment. Both major parties supported it as early as 1944, but organized labor and most women leaders prevented it from being in either of their party platforms in both 1964 and 1968.[34]

The 1920s feminist believed she had won; her goals had been achieved. "Today there are few pursuits which women do not follow with more or less success. The opportunities are almost unlimited"—so said one, and another, a woman lawyer, predicted that by the 1950s there would be no sex prejudice at all.[35] But these women did not reckon with the fact that nature—God's natural order—cannot be undone by laws, movements, or even ideologies. The male-female polarity continued to exercise a strong "magnetic" pull on how people lived, so much so that on the eve of World War II, some 20 years after the great changes of the '20s, "the patterns of women's work were remarkably similar to what they had been at the end of the 19th century..."[36]

It took a world war to shake up the male-female polarity significantly. To support the war effort during World War II, the government needed female workers. But while 33 percent of childless wives would work, only nineteen percent of those with children would, and only 30 percent of the husbands thought it was acceptable to have their wives working. This was a crisis to the federal government, so it began a propaganda campaign on its own citizens, "to convince married women, including those with small children, that it was now patriotic to work outside the home."[37] But even four years of patriotically working outside of the home did not change public opinion or the male-female polarity. After World War II a 1945 poll found that 63 percent of Americans thought women should not work if the husband could support her and that child-rearing was to be her main job.[38]

Even after the extreme conditions brought on by a world at war, the male-female polarity survived. "Indeed, aside from the National Women's Party, which was minuscule in membership, there was no truly feminist organization in the whole country. Right down until the late 1960s, in fact, 'feminist' was a dirty word, redolent of old maids, 'blue-stockings,' and 'man-haters.'"[39] Right up until the 1970s, although more and more women were entering the work force, the majority of women were still found in occupations that were similar to those they held in 1940 or even 1900.[40]

Modern feminism, at least for popular consumption at the pew level, came on the scene in the form of Friedan's book, *The Feminine Mystique*. The basic thesis of this book is that women are miserable because they are trying to fill the roles that men have placed them in for the benefit of men. Men keep women in their place through the power of religion, economics, and reproduction.

The rest of this book will deal with the issues raised by Friedan. For now, the present author simply wants to relate how Friedan herself says this work came about:

> I have never experienced anything as powerful, truly mystical, as the forces that seemed to take me over when I was writing *The Feminine Mystique*. The book came from somewhere deep within me and all my experience came together in it; my mother's discontent, my own training in Gestalt and Freudian psychology, ...my exodus to the suburbs and all the hours with other mothers shopping at supermarkets, taking the children swimming, coffee klatches...Even the years of writing for women's magazines when it was unquestioned gospel that women could identify

> with nothing beyond the home... After I finished each
> chapter, a part of me would wonder, Am I crazy?[41]

We noted earlier that according to Friedan what brought about the woman movement in 1848 was a woman being discontent with the drudgery of being a housewife after being on the front lines of the abolitionist movement. Now we find out that what brought about the resurgence and the ultimate popularization of feminism was a woman being discontent with the drudgery of being a housewife after having sampled the heady atmosphere of the world. But there is another similarity between the two. The 1848 movement was heavily influenced by Quakers who rely on an "inner light" for revelation. Friedan says she was influenced by "forces that seemed to take her over."

Matters progressed rapidly after 1963 due mainly to the Civil Rights Act of 1964. This act was not originally intended to speak to the women's issue, but a Southern congressman, seeking to make the bill more difficult to pass, added "sex" in addition to color, race, religion, and national origin as not being a reason to discriminate. President Johnson took him by complete surprise when he came out in favor of that addition. In the studied opinion of historian Professor Carl Degler, "The Civil Rights Act of 1964 was surely the most significant single force behind the new feminist movement, for from then on women's equality of opportunity was endorsed by the Federal government."[42]

With the sanction of the government behind their cause, the first truly feminist organization since the National Women's Party over 50 years earlier was formed. The National Organization for Women (NOW) was founded by Friedan herself using royalties from *The Feminine Mystique*. This group drafted a "Bill of Rights for Women" in 1967. Its two most radical goals were advocacy for the Equal Rights Amendment and "the right of women to control their reproductive lives." At that time abortion was illegal in every state unless the life of the mother was in danger.[43]

The feminist tide rolled on. In 1969, Cornell became the first college to have a women's studies program.[44] In 1983, the United States Department of Education gave formal recognition to "Women's Studies" as a degree speciality.[45] Now there is no major college that does not have a Women's Studies program, if not department. But it is not just academia that is awash in feminism; so is everyday language. "Ms." was introduced at the feminist counterpart to "Mr." at a 1969 NOW conference. But a Virginia Slims American Women's Opinion Poll reported that 77 percent of women preferred the designation "Miss" or "Mrs."[46] Now who does not use the term "Ms."? It has all but eclipsed the use of "Miss" and "Mrs."

In the eighteenth century, women demanded, quite rightly, that men do everything they could to exalt the roles of wife and mother. They wanted men to help women be better wives and mothers. They gloried in the differences between men women. In the nineteenth century, the "woman movement" demanded equality of men and women, arguing both from the differences and the sameness of men and women. The twentieth century feminist has boldly demanded equality to the point of interchangeability, arguing that socialization *alone* caused the inequality. Some have even gone so far as to claim superiority over men. But nature—God's created polarity—will not be hidden. Books such as the recent (1993) Why Men Rule (which does not argue from a religious point of view) firmly established that men and women are not interchangeable and that, physically speaking, men always have and always will dominate.

But feminism is far from dead—or even wounded. It is going back to its nineteenth century roots and claiming that women are superior spiritually. However, some new wrinkles have been added. Men now are said to need women's spirituality to fully understand God or to get in contact with him/her. This new wrinkle can be as blatant as witchcraft and goddess worship or as subtle as implying that men and women are so different spiritually that they will relate to God differently and, therefore, have different, yet equally valid, interpretations of God's Word. Basically what is happening is that New Age spirituality is blossoming within feminism, and once more man is being asked by woman to follow her down a path that is soft, sweet, and delicious, a veritable delight to all the senses. But this path, too, only leads out of the garden.

How did we get on this path? Why have we stayed on it? Why is feminism so hard to resist? These questions are especially troubling in light of the fact that there has been an all but unanimous rejection of the tenets of feminism from the earliest days of Christianity right up until now. Christianity faced the theology of feminism from the beginning; it took on a pagan world devoted to the Mother goddess under various names.[47] Even from within the ranks of Christianity, the early church faced feminist theologizing as offered by Montanism and Gnosticism. While not a feminist movement *per se*, Arianism stirred up women: 700 single women were among the first to support Arius' contention that deity should not be ascribed to Christ.

Montanism was an apocalyptic movement of the late second century. (It would not be far afield to characterize it as the first Pentecostal movement.) Montanus "prophesied" ca. 170 A.D.; he traveled with two female assistants; both had deserted husbands and one had a vision of Christ as a female.[48] Modern feminists have also had such "visions," even going so far as to sculpt a female Christ crucified. Montanism had female bishops and priests and claimed, just as modern day feminists do, Galatians 3:28 as justification for their departure from apostolic practice.[49] It is interesting to note that a hallmark of late nineteenth and early twentieth century Pentecostals was giving the pulpit to women.

Gnosticism was more of a force to be dealt with by the early Church than Montanism was. Gnostics claimed to have a higher knowledge given to them by a special revelation that superseded the Bible. They also claimed to have a higher form of faith in which the distinctions between male and female were not recognized. Gnostic gods were all masculo-feminine according to Irenaeus in *Against Heresies*.[50] The Gnostic notion was that in generation the male deity gave the *form*, but the female deity provided the *substance*.[51] Deborah Belonick, a self-confessed Christian feminist, has this to say concerning the relationship between Gnosticism and feminism, "Among such Gnostic groups as the Valentinians, for example, the female divinity supported women's equality to men. Many women in such groups were prophets, teachers, traveling evangelists, healers, priests, and perhaps even bishops."[52]

The early Church knew feminist thinking *via* Gnosticism and responded by writing against it. The *Didascalia Apostolorum* (ca. 245 A.D.) argues against women being pastors from the fact that Jesus could have chosen and commissioned women as apostles but did not.[53]

The *Constitutions of the Holy Apostles* (dating to ca. 380 A.D.) firmly, precisely, and Scripturally rejects the practices and principles that pass as "modern" feminism today:

> We do not permit our 'women to teach in the Church,' but only to pray and hear those that teach; for our Master and Lord, Jesus Himself, when He sent us the twelve to make disciples of the people and of the nations, did nowhere send out women to preach, although He did not want [lack] such....For 'if the head of the wife be the man,' it is not reasonable that the rest of the body should govern the head.[54]

Three chapters later we read:

> Now, as to women's baptizing, we let you know that there is no small peril to those that undertake it. Therefore we do not advise you to it; for it is dangerous, rather wicked and impious. For if the 'man be

the head of the woman,' and he be originally ordained for the priesthood, it is not just to abrogate the order of creation, and leaven the principal to come to the extreme part of the body. For the woman is the body of the man, taken from his side, and subject to him, from whom she was separated for the procreation of children....But if in the foregoing constitutions we have not permitted them to teach, how will any one allow them, contrary to nature, to perform the office of a priest? For this is one of the ignorant practices of Gentile atheism, to ordain women priests to the female deities, not one of the constitutions of Christ.[55]

There are warnings from the Lutheran fathers, too. In his exegesis of Psalm 2, Martin Luther says, "For it is character-istic of all heretics, hypocrites, and sects to devise some other picture of God for themselves."[56] Another Lutheran father, Martin Chemnitz, warned already in 1570 about a favorite tool of modern feminists. He said, "[I]f, because of unexplainable absurdities, we are forced to depart from the clear word of God, nothing will remain safe among the chief articles of our faith."[57] While not a father of the Lutheran church, Professor W.H.T. Dau's words of warning found in a 1916 work en-titled *Woman Suffrage in the Church* were deemed worthy to be preserved in a history of the Lutheran Church—Missouri Synod published in 1964:

The emancipation of woman, sex equality, and all that is connected with these fundamental ideas have gone so far throughout the world that it seems impossible that there will be turning back. Thoughtful men are dreading the feministic movement of our times, principally for the women's sake. In the long run it will be found that the movement has not elevated or liberated woman, but lowered and shackled her, and the chains which the "free" woman will bear will be worse than any she was supposed to bear in the past....If the secular state for reason of its own adopts woman suffrage the church for reasons of its own may decline the same. Each follows its own authority and standard.[58]

The outcry against the assumptions, principles, goals and practices of feminism has been sounding in the Church for over a millennium; in the past fifteen years it has reached a veritable crescendo. Yet the Church has appeased, conceded, surrendered. Has she perhaps converted? Is the Bride of Christ now a Ms.? Why is feminism so hard to resist? Listening to the articulate, consistent hue and cry against feminism that has sounded in the Church in the last fifteen years, one has to ask: how could it be to no avail?

In 1980 Stephen Clark published his exhaustive work, *Man and Woman in Christ*. In it, Clark answered decisively some of the most frequent arguments feminists have raised in support of their position. For example, feminists say that Jesus introduced a radically new way of treating women that did away with role distinctions. Clark answered:

> The fact that he did treat women very well, with love and respect, is by no means incompatible with acceptance of role differences between men and women. Only someone who believes that genuine love and respect must be incompatible with role differentiation would be able to detect a revolutionary intent in Jesus' behavior despite the lack of evidence for it.[59]

The feminists say Paul's epistles only give Paul's opinion about male and female roles, and since Paul had a bad attitude towards women, his opinion is not valid today. Clark answered: "There is more evidence for Paul's friendship with women than for Jesus' and more examples of the way Paul 'furthered' the woman's role than of how Jesus did this."[60] Besides,

> The fact that the New Testament teaching on roles

is Pauline and not explicitly from Jesus is no reason to call into question its authentic Christianity. One could just as logically reconsider the circumcision question because only Paul left explicit teaching on the subject. The teaching of the "key texts" arises in the context of the "Pauline" environment of the mission to the Gentiles and to the Jews who lived among them because those were the Christians who needed to hear such teaching.[61]

And to us who have appeased, conceded, and receded in the area of the roles of men and women, Clark warned:

If this teaching can be dispensed with considering its backing in Scripture and tradition, then there is no prescription of the government of the Christian people than cannot likewise be put aside....If this teaching can by changed by Christians, there is very little that cannot be changed.[62]

Clark was not alone in warning where feminism would take us. Many in the Church are shocked and amazed by the rapid rise and open acceptance of homosexuality in the last ten years, but fourteen years ago Elisabeth Elliot told us:

It is extremely important to note that once the first premise of feminism is conceded (that sexual difference is merely physiological, rather than theological) it is reasonable to conclude that men and women may express "sexual preference." Where the very nature and meaning of sexuality is lost, it becomes a matter of taste rather than principle.[63]

Even a Seventh Day Adventist, with a long history of following female leadership, rose to the occasion and rebuked feminism answering feminist arrogance on two counts. To feminists who wanted to tout modern role interchangeability over "archaic" role distinctions, Samuele Bacchiocchi responded in 1987: "The underlying belief that the modern social pattern of role interchangeability is more true than the ancient Biblical pattern of role distinctions is a gratuitous assumption."[64] To feminist scholars who believed local conditions called forth Paul's remarks about women, and therefore, they should not be applied to today, he responded:

> The fact that a particular teaching was occasioned by local circumstances does not per se negate the normative nature of such a teaching. Paul's teaching that 'a man is not justified by the works of the law but through faith in Jesus Christ' (Gal. 2:16) is not regarded as lacking universal validity because it was occasioned by a specific Judaizing heresy which attracted the Galatians. The general applicability of virtually any Biblical command could be negated simply by arguing that there are possible local circumstances behind it.[65]

From within the Lutheran church, there has been no lack of voices raised in opposition to feminist thinking. In his 1991 dogmatics work, Professor Kurt Marquart clearly rejects the deepest of feminist errors, thereby rejecting all the shallower ones as well. He says, "A church which ordains women certifies itself to be un-apostolic and anti-apostolic."[66]

Roman Catholic journalist Donna Steichen warned of the feminism's connection has with Satanism and witchcraft. "Feminism appears to be the bait, moral disintegration the hook and the occult the dark and treacherous sea into which the deluded are towed."[67] Four years ago, Steichen would not allow the relatively tame labels of "schism" and "heresy" on feminism. No she said, "It is an apostasy to an alien religion."[68]

Another Christian woman—this time a Baptist—also sounded a wake up call in the Church in 1992. Mary Kassian warned that feminist theologians were attacking the only objective means we have for knowing God by declaring that

36

the language of faith which reveals God as Father and God as Son concealed rather than revealed the true God.[69] Feminist theologians consider masculine pronouns to be inadequate for describing God. Kassian warned also of the danger of making a distinction between secular and religious feminism. "The themes of religious feminism were, in essence, identical to the themes of secular feminism. However, these themes were shrouded by remnants of Christian imagery and language."[70] For example, a Christian feminist might choose to use masculine pronouns for God even though she "knew" they were inadequate. Kassian was clear in warning us that it was impossible to have both feminism and Christianity. "Feminism is, to the evangelical church, a watershed issue. In order to introduce feminist concepts into Christianity, basic beliefs regarding the inspiration and authority of Scripture need to be adjusted."[71]

Finally, we have Christian testimony about the danger of feminism from 1994. Alan Morrison warned that feminism is endemic to fallen humanity. "God was never a woman; people just imagined He was. Perhaps we can now understand why God has put such checks on women, both in His judgement in the wake of the Fall (Gen. 3:18) and through His apostles in the early church (I Tim. 2:9-15)."[72] And Morrison exposed the same satanic malevolence behind feminism that Steichen warned of years earlier. "The stark truth is that Feminism is not, and has never been, about the attainment of equality for women but the seizing of superiority over men—all in fulfillment of Satan's desire to invert God's prescribed order."[73]

The Church has been warned from within many, many times, but she has also been warned from without; voices outside of the Church expressed concerns regarding feminism and its desire to deny role distinctions. We now turn to these warnings.

In 1922 Frank Wile, a Philadelphia journalist, observed: "...Uncle Sam will wake up one morning to discover that long-haired men and short-haired women have enthroned themselves in the place where patriotic intelligence once prevailed."[74] While Mr. Wile was a journalist not a prophet, seventy-six years later one has to admit he was right. Regardless of what hairstyles they wear, both feminized men and masculinized women are acceptable and frequently they are in power. This secular journalist saw trouble coming from feminism a long way off, and he gave due warning.

So did others. In a speech in 1926, Secretary of Labor James Davis said that the great danger of the age was the "increasing loss of the distinction between manliness and true femininity."[75] Secular anthropologist Margaret Mead, certainly no Christian apologist, also gave the Church a warning. She said,

> If any human society—large or small, simple or complex, based on the most rudimentary hunting and fishing or on the whole intricate interchange of manufactured products—is to survive, it must have a pattern of social life that comes to terms with the differences between the sexes.[76]

More recently a Christian author added the observation that, "*If a 'unisexual' world is unnatural, only force can maintain it, only failure and misery can accompany it.*"[77] This is why we have lawyers forcing the doors of the Citadel open. This is why we have different physical fitness standards Army-wide for men and women that hide the fact that women cannot compete with men. Columnist John Leo remarked in a 1997 article:

> But the chief reason for change is the return of mixed-gender training, which the Army tried for several years, abandoned as a failure in 1982, and reinstalled under feminist political pressure in 1994....Reconfiguring basic training so that "anybody could get through" was largely a response to women's high rate of injury and inability to meet the old standards.[78]

Secular authors see the insanity of feminism; they may even see it more clearly than the Church does. Certainly they have a better grasp of the incredible societal ramifications feminist thinking has had on all of us. Consider the remarks of this social scientist:

> Our young are the first people of whom the following can be said: if they are males, they and their fathers and their brothers and sons and all the males they know are overwhelmingly likely to have been reared under the direct domination and supervision of females from birth to maturity. No less important is the fact that their mothers and their sisters and their girl friends and their wives and all of the ladies with whom they have had to do have had to do only with males so reared....To put the matter as dramatically as possible, we do not even know whether viable human beings can over any long period of time be reared in such a fashion. After all, this has never held true of any substantial proportion of any population for even one generation in the history of the world until the last fifty years.[79]

Another writer explains how it came to be that women have such an exclusive role in rearing boys. She points out that it has only been that way since the nineteenth century, and it is only here in America that the majority of grade school teachers in public and private schools are women.[80] Unfortunately, boys do not learn to be men from women.

Even those outside of the Church know that feminism has had a profoundly negative impact on society as a whole. New York Post columnist Don Feder said in a September 27, 1987 column, "The true misogynists (woman-haters) are feminists—despising as they do, all of the unique characteristics of womankind." The characteristics feminists particularly despise are those that make women gifted for homemaking and child-rearing. Senator Sam Ervin saw in the '70s that feminism had its "gun sights" set on these things. Speaking against the ERA he pleaded for the law to support the order which God established: "on the man to bear the burdens of support and the woman to bear the children."[81] The senator saw what social analyst Peter Druker did in 1982: "We are busily unmaking one of the proudest social achievements in the nineteenth century, which was to take married women out of the work force so they could devote themselves to family and children."[82]

Even some of the original advocates of the rights of women did not want to see the dismantling which has come to pass. A defender of working women, economist Helen Cambell said, "The employment of married women is fruitful of evil." In 1912, another friend of working women, Earl Barnes said, "Surely the ideal toward which we must work... is for the mother, during the period she is bearing and rearing children, to be supported by the father of her children." John Stuart Mill, an early feminist, wrote in his 1869 work, *The Subjection of Women*, that it was not a desirable custom for the wife to contribute her labor to the family income. And almost one hundred years later (1964) the Women's Bureau officially announced it was not its policy, "to encourage married women and mothers of young children to seek employment outside the home. Home and children are considered married women's most important responsibilities."[83]

The first colleges for women were founded for the purpose of making women better homemakers and mothers. Even as late as 1925, the president of Skidmore College said in his inaugural speech, "One of the chief ends of college for women is to fit them to become the makers of home; whatever else a woman may be, the highest purpose of her life always has been to strengthen and beautify and sanctify the home."[84]

People in secular society realize that feminism is a denial of reality. It is more than a denial; it is a fight against empirical reality. A former Army officer who experienced the ravages of feminism firsthand in the military calls feminism, "the disastrous triumph of ideology over reality."[85]

The reality of the relationship between the sexes, as even secularists point out, comes through in the arts, despite the feminist attack. For example, young, idealistic feminists sought to change the romance novel industry. Young editors, steeped in feminist assumptions during college, sought out only "politically correct" writers who were willing to do away with the "alpha-male" aggressive hero and heroines who were almost always sexually-inexperienced virgins. These writers bombed.[86]

God's gender polarity wins out. Secular sociologist Steven Goldberg sees this; contrary to the prevailing feminist assumption, he asserts,

> [T]he male strength and dominance and the female gentleness and endurance portrayed in our novels and movies mirror not merely our society's view of the emotional natures of men and women, but the views of every society that has ever existed.[87]
>
> ...If the few remaining laws that differentiate between the sexes are removed, it will become clear in time that such laws had merely reflected society's acknowledgment of sexual differences but had not caused them.[88]

From all around the Church—not just from within her—the cry has gone up throughout the last fifteen years that men and women were made, created, or even evolved differently. Even though secular authorities were wrong on the origin of the male-female polarity—citing evolution rather than creation—they still recognized the polarity exists. Still, this recognition was present much longer than fifteen years ago.

Historian Carl Degler has conducted extensive research concerning the life of women on the American frontier. He cites a study done by two historians (one female) which concluded that, "women fought against the forces of necessity to hold together the few fragments of female subculture left to them."[89] Women wanted to be women even in the very masculine situation of crossing the country by wagon train. Degler notes that while women would take on very masculine tasks during the trip, the first-person accounts clearly show they did so with great reluctance.[90] He also notes that the nineteenth century utopian communities which ignored the rules of gender segregation attracted few women.[91]

Even John Stuart Mill recognized the tremendous power of nature. In his *The Subjection of Women* (1869), he acknowledged the pull of gender polarity, saying, "One thing we may be certain of—that what is contrary to women's nature to do, they never will be made to do by simply giving their nature free play."[92] Mills warned us over 125 years ago that only *force* could bring about a change in gender roles.

Betty Friedan, the mother of modern day feminism, at least had the courage to admit that is was not men who forced women into certain roles but women who chose them. In *The Feminine Mystique*, Friedan wrestles with why women who were released from the home through 1920s feminism and then by World War II went back into the home. She concludes, "In the last analysis, millions of able women in this free land chose themselves, not to use the door education could have opened for them. The choice—and the responsibility—for the race back home was finally their own."[93]

The real tenacity of gender polarity is not seen here in America; it is seen in those cultures which have tried to neutralize it. The former Soviet Union, the People's Republic of China, and the Israeli Kibbutzim all embraced radical programs intended to neutralize or even nullify the masculine-feminine polarity created by God. Despite decades of indoctrination, not one of these cultures has succeeded.[94]

Probably the strongest way the male-female polarity expresses itself is through the institution of patriarchy. Every culture, society, and family system has been patriarchal. This should not surprise anyone who believes that God knew what He was doing when He created Adam and Eve in the manner and order that He did and gave them the roles that He did. But this reality rankles the feminists. In spite of this, secular authorities still testify to the universality of patriarchy.

George Gilder flatly states, "males in all societies ever studied by anthropologists overwhelmingly prevail in positions of leadership and hold authority in relations with women."[95] Sociologist Stephen Goldberg declares, "authority and leadership are, and always have been, associated with the male in every society."[96] Furthermore, no society or group anywhere ever associates authority with a female if there is a male of equal rank available.[97] Throughout his work, *Why Men Rule*, Goldberg asserts and defends the fact that men rule in all societies in a non-biblical, non-Christian, non-religious way. Please note: he doesn't defend the proposition that men *should* rule; as a sociologist, his interest is accurately reporting what the facts show.

Writing long after feminism had swept the country, Goldberg makes a startling conclusion: "every society recognizes a particular emotional difference between men and women, and that this difference always works in the same direction." The direction is: men tell women, women ask men; men do, women are allowed; and men lead, women follow.[98] In another place, Goldberg makes a pointedly-un-feminist conclusion: "The number of women in the highest positions of leadership and authority varies from zero to perhaps six or seven percent as one spans the entire range of human societies—including those societies in which women comprise half the work force."[99] His conclusion is borne out in a small way when one considers the lay delegates to the 1995 Lutheran Church—Missouri Synod convention. The 1,156 voting delegates represented some 6,000 congregations whose membership totaled 2.5 million. Of these, 67 (5.8 percent) were female. This is the result that Goldberg would expect, even though this particular church body has had decades of propaganda concerning the crises of women in the Church and how their input and leadership are desperately needed at the highest levels of the Church.

Patriarchy is universal and inevitable, according to Goldberg's *Why Men Rule*. This is the conclusion of someone *outside* of the Church; what would happen if this conclusion was repeated loudly inside the Church? The same tired feminist arguments would be dragged out in response. Those doing the dragging may or may not be feminists—they merely repeat the assumptions with which they have been inoculated, perhaps without even knowing it.

"What about the Amazons?," someone might say or, "What about this or that culture which Margaret Mead proved was matriarchal?" We admit that there are matri*local* cultures (where lineages are traced through mothers) and matrifocal ones (where the female role receives special honor and attention), but, supported by many secular experts, we would have to deny there was ever such a thing as truly matri*archal* culture.[100] Goldberg alone could be sufficient authority on this point, since he cites every culture that is alleged to be an exception to the universality of patriarchy and male dominance. He tells us, "I have read many claims of societies that are exceptions to the universals we discuss [patriarchy and male dominance]. In not one case is the claim made by the anthropologists who actually studied the society in question."[101]

If we are not satisfied with a male "authority" such as Goldberg, we could turn to a female. Anthropologist Margaret Mead wrote in a 1973 *Redbook* article,

> It is true...that all the claims so glibly made about societies ruled by women are nonsense. We have no reason to believe that they ever existed....[M]en everywhere have been in charge of running the show.... [M]en have been the leaders in public affairs and the final authorities at home.[102]

   With such a clear statement that matriarchal societies do not exist, you would think no one would cite Mead to the contrary any longer. But thirty out of thirty-two sociological textbooks checked in 1990 referenced Margaret Mead and her research of the Tchambuli society as proof that sex-role reversal can happen, despite the fact that for forty years Mead denied that a sex-role reversal had occurred in that society. The offending college textbooks erroneously used the Tchambuli society to prove that society caused sex roles.[103] In other words, they used it as "proof" that there was no such thing as a God-given gender polarity.

   But what about the Amazons? What about those whom Homer styled the "women peers of men?"[104] As late as December 1971, *Time* magazine was reporting that they existed; there had been an all-women, lesbian tribe which raided male tribes to mate and then killed the males. *Time* reported that the proof of their existence was the ideograms they left behind in Brazil. Now, of course, the fact that the alleged Amazonian societies never existed has been proven by a number of anthropologists.[105] Abby Weltan Kleinbaum spent ten years researching the subject for her book, *The War Against the Amazons*; she concluded they never existed.[106]

   The fact that the Amazons never were real is not the important thing to remember; the fact that they were invented is. The Greeks and the Romans made up the Amazon stories for the same reason people today make up science fiction: for entertainment and for satisfaction. An Amazon culture was entertaining because it was so far removed from the realm of the probable or even the possible. Also, like science fiction sometimes does, the Amazon stories satisfied man's sinful desire for what is perverse or base. Sinful man, and Satan himself (as was pointed out earlier), love to see God's created order toppled, if only in their imaginations.

   The ancient Amazons were not real, but modern feminism aims to produce them by their drive to neutralize the masculine-feminine polarity in society, church, and home. Authorities outside of the home are warning us of this. The 1985 landmark study, *Habits of the Heart* (which has been compared to Tocqueville's *Democracy in America* in terms of its in-depth look at American society), warns us of the coming of the Amazons. Based on interviews across America done over a five year time period, the authors state: "There is an anxiety, not without foundation, among some of the opponents of feminism, that the equality of women could result in complete loss of the human qualities long associated with 'women's sphere.'"[107] George Gilder warns of the result if this happens: "Aggressive and competitive women, unconcerned with motherhood, produce more ruthless men..."[108] While boys do not learn to be men from women, they do not learn to be socially productive men without them.

Amazingly enough, Jean Jacques Rousseau saw this trouble coming hundreds of years ago. According to Will and Ariel Durant, "Rousseau feared masculine, domineering, immodest women; he saw the fall of civilization in the rule of increasingly masculine women over increasingly feminine men." Through a series of quotes, the Durants outlined Rousseau's view:

> In every land the men are the sort that the women make them;....[R]estore women to womanhood, and we shall be men again....The women of Paris usurp the rights of one sex without wishing to renounce those of the other; consequently they possess none in their fullness.[109]

There is a war going on. It is a war against masculinity and femininity. What is going to result is not androgyny or matriarchy but anarchy. What we are going to lose is not masculinity but true masculinity. What we will have instead is masculinity gone berserk—barbarity. What we will lose is femininity. Women will be forced to compete with men, and it will be much the same in all walks of a life as it is in athletics. "Unlike men who succeed in athletics largely in proportion to their manliness—by perfecting their male bodies—women succeed by suppressing their femininity and imitating men."[110] Serious women athletes interfere with their menstrual cycle by their excessive working out; some have even stopped the cycle.

An incident that has to do with the American frontier illustrates what society will lose if we lose femininity. A granddaughter went to the nursing home to collect the personal belongings of her grandmother who had been a pioneer on the Great Plains in the nineteenth century. The personal possessions of this pioneer woman, because of many moves and necessity, had been distilled to their very essence. Therefore what the granddaughter found at the nursing home was a few photographs, a wedding ring, an immigration certificate, newspaper clippings about her son's distinguished military service, and a small wooden box. Inside was the small, dehydrated body of a canary that had been dead a very long time. This canary had been the pioneer woman's companion out on the desolate plains. If you look at old photos of pioneer homesteader's, you will see a tired, dirty family in front of a sod home. In the background hanging from the eves, you will often see a bird cage. If you look hard, you can even make out a canary.[111]

Only femininity would think of bringing beauty, song, and delicateness to such a desolate and hostile environment. Aside from the theological havoc feminism will doubtlessly wreak on the Church, society will suffer the loss of the beautifiers of this fallen, barren world. Even secular thinkers can see this, and they have warned us.

The Church has been warned about feminism by secular society and by the feminists themselves; they warned us not only by their words and deeds but by their backgrounds. The first women to take up the cause of feminism were, for the most part, notorious. This is not merely the author's judgment, but it is also the conclusion of others. Fanny Wright and Ernestine

Rose were the first women to speak up for 'women's rights' in America. At the time (c. 1820s), Fanny Wright was referred to as the "red harlot of infidelity," and Ernestine Rose was called the "woman a thousand times below a prostitute."[112]

Betty Friedan bristles when she reports this, seeing such name-calling as typical of how outspoken women were vilified in the press. In Wright's case, however, the label seems accurate. In an age of religion, Wright advocated less church-going for women and had no religion at all in her utopian community called Nashoba. In an age where marriage was held in high regard, she had a questionable relationship with General Lafayette, a man old enough to be her father. And after starting her utopian community, she publicly declared that outside marriage laws had no force inside the community. As a consequence, it was labeled a "free love colony."[113]

Both church and society should have been warned of where feminism would lead by the likes of Victoria Woodhull, an outspoken suffragist and proponent of radical marriage re-form. In the 1870s, she proudly proclaimed that she followed love wherever it led her, and, though married, she lived openly with another man. In response to those who said that she had come to break up marriage she once remarked, "I say amen to that with all my heart."[114] So when Gloria Steinem said in a 1977 speech, "For the sake of those who wish to live in equal partnership, we have to abolish and reform the institution of marriage,"[115] why were we so surprised? That had been a goal of some feminists for over 100 years!

Not just the words and deeds of feminists, but their very backgrounds should have been a warning to us. When reading the biographies of the founding "mothers" of femi-nism in Rossi's *The Feminist Papers*, one cannot help but sense something is wrong. Many, if not most, of them came from shattered or unusual backgrounds. Rossi cites, although she does not agree with it, a 1947 work which reached this same conclusion: "Mary Wollstonecraft's [the eighteenth century matriarch of feminism] life reads like a psychiatric case history. So, for that matter, do the lives, of many later feminists..."[116] This same work is of the opinion that it was out of Wollstonecraft's illness that the ideology of feminism arose.[117] This is not a promising pedigree.

Our forefathers and foremothers tried to warn us of the dangers of feminism. Most of the warnings came from the anti-suffrage movement, which was mostly made up of women. In 1913 a tract from the Missouri Anti-Suffrage League warned, "Feminism advocates non-motherhood, free love, easy divorce, economic independence for all women, and other demoralizing and destructive theories."[118]

The 1916 Republican presidential candidate, Charles Evans Hughs, was against feminism. He worried about a "distinct feminist movement constantly perfecting its organization to the subversion of normal political issues."[119] Were his worries justified? It seems so. Normal political issues such as defense, commerce, and taxation have come to take a "back seat" to such women's issues as abortion, sexual harassment, the gender gap, the "glass ceiling," federally-funded day care, maternity leave, date rape, women in combat, etc.

We were warned, but we did not listen. For example, many today are concerned with the distinctly socialist turn our country has taken. In 1918, the Anti-Suffrage League in Missouri warned us by asking rhetorically, "Do you know that there is a close alliance between woman suffrage, Socialism, and Feminism; that Feminism advocates non-motherhood, free love, easy divorce, economic independence for all women, and other demoralizing and destructive theories?"[120] Almost eighty years later we have abortion on demand, a fertility rate incapable of even maintaining our population, forty percent of couples cohabiting prior to marriage, no-fault divorce laws, and a welfare society that can only be funded by the redistribution of wealth.

Though the history of feminism is filled with extreme

ideas concerning marriage, sexuality, society, and family, for the most part there were two areas that were almost sacrosanct even among feminists: childbearing and mothering. Historically, the majority of feminists did not attack these two areas. It was not until 1963 that Betty Friedan attacked mothering as being unfulfilling, demeaning, enslaving, and even retarding. By doing so, she broke what F. Carolyn Graglia has called the "Women's Pact." Graglia insists there have always been women who did not seek to be mothers, but the unwritten "pact" was that women did not attack each other for the path they chose: mothers did not attack career women for not staying at home and career women did not attack mothers for staying at home.[121]

Betty Friedan attacked mothering, but even she (in the beginning) did not dare attack the hallowed ground of childbearing—this was left for later feminists. The early feminists, prior to Betty Friedan, were aware that childbearing and mothering were absolutely essential for society to continue, let alone prosper. For this reason, most of the leaders of the woman movement who led the battle and achieved the victory of suffrage rejected the ERA that followed three years later. They opposed it, "on the ground that it was harmful to women, their essential nature, and their place in society."[122]

By "essential nature" nothing less was meant than their ability to bring new life into society. Labor unions and industry as a whole also believed women had a special role and place. Historically, labor laws placed women with children, not because women were childish but because women should be afforded special protection by the law even as children should be. In 1900 the American Federation of Labor said women should be lumped with children, "because it is to the interest of all of us that female labor should be limited so as to not injure the motherhood and family life of a nation."[123]

To be sure, the labor unions argued at other times for restricting women's labor for the sake of preserving jobs for men. Throughout the history of feminism, feminists point out this dual way in which men argue: women should be in a special class for the benefit of men; women should be in a special class for the protection of women and society. But before one comes down too hard on men, it must be recognized that women have argued out of both sides of their mouths, too. Women have said they should be given special privileges because they are women and different than men, and, simultaneously, women have said they should be treated the same as men because they are not different from men. Confronted by these two arguments, men have the choice of being insensitive or sexist, depending out of which side of the mouth the feminist is speaking.

The feminists of the 1920s also wanted women protected because of their unique roll as mothers. Florence Kelly, former member of the National Women's Party, said in 1922 that as long as men cannot be mothers, "so long legislation adequate for them can never be adequate for wage-earning women; and the cry Equality, Equality, where Nature had created Inequality, is as stupid and as deadly as the cry Peace, Peace where there is no peace."[124]

And a leader in the League of Women Voters said in 1926 that the majority of women,

> believe that the most important function of woman in the world is motherhood, that the welfare of the child should be the first consideration, and that because of their maternal functions women should be protected against undue strain.[125]

The notion has arisen that women should come before children. Without specifically saying it, feminists are the first to champion that hallowed principle of psychology: "If you don't take care of yourself first, you can't take care of anyone else." Contrast this modern and still very popular self-centered view with "ardent feminist" Eva Von Baur Hansl's view in the

1920s. She fervently believed that a woman had every right to pursue any career she chose; however, there was a catch: "But to this I would add the corollary that when she chooses to bring children into this world, they have a prior claim upon her attention."[126]

Childbearing and mothering—these were glorious privileges given to women even in the eyes of the early feminists. Mary Wollstonecraft, the eighteenth century matriarch of feminism, said that the woman's sphere was related to her maternal character, and that a women's duties were, "to manage a family or to educate children" without complaining.[127] Writing as late as 1902, radical feminist and anarchist Emma Goldman could call the ability to give birth to children a woman's "most glorious privilege."[128]

The early feminists did not start out attacking childbearing or mothering. Modern day feminism did not start out attacking them, either. Now, of course, neither are sacred except on Mother's Day. So what is a woman to do or to be? What is the point of her life? Where is meaning to be found for her? The stabilizers of society have been made very unstable by feminism. Anthropologist Margaret Mead warns us of the danger of this, saying that the recurrent problem of civilization has always been to define the male role. The female role did not need defining; it was outlined by biology (until modern times the Church would have unashamedly said by God through biology), and therefore females serve to stabilize every civilization. Mead emphasizes the stability of women by saying, "If women are to be restless and questioning, even in the face of childbearing, they must be made so through education."[129]

This is exactly what happened with many feminists right down to Betty Friedan. Education "opened" their minds to the enduring question of Satan, "Is this all there is?" They have boldly answered "No!," even going so far as to say that mothering may not be worth the time for some women; therefore, by deduction neither may childbearing. So women have been raised since the 1960s with the belief that meaning, destiny, purpose, fulfillment are not to be sought where God Himself ordained them to be for women. But for modern women this does not have to be "educated" out of the divinely-ordained plan as women were prior to the 1960s; today it is "assumed" out of them. Women naturally assume that meaning, purpose, and fulfillment are not to be found in childbearing and mothering. Of course, one might say yesterday's women only assumed it was found there. The issue is: which assumptions are biblical? Historically, the assumptions of feminists have not been considered biblical. Friedan herself testifies to this saying, "At every step of the way, the feminists had to fight the conception that they were violating the God-given nature of women."[130]

Feminists did warn us that the very things they ended up attacking, childbearing and mothering, were critical to the well-being of society. They also warned us about another facet of the male-female polarity that is much maligned, attacked, and even denied today: subordination. The feminists cited below vary as to how they explain it and even as to how they see it, but they all admit to seeing this subordination.

John Stuart Mill, nineteenth century feminist advocate, admitted that the subjection of women to men was a universal custom.[131] An ex-feminist of the 1920s said that feminine subordination was expedient.[132] In her 1949 book, *The Second Sex*, Simone de Beauvoir argued against subordination being only the result of circumstances. "Throughout history they have always been subordinated to men, and hence their dependency is not the result of a historical event or a social change—it was not something that occurred."[133]

Modern day feminist scholar Sherry Ortner also testifies concerning subordination:

> I would flatly assert that we find women subordinate to men in every known society. The search for a genuinely

egalitarian, let alone matriarchal, culture has proved fruitless....The universality of female subordination, the fact that it exists within every type of social and economic arrangement and in societies of every degree of complexity, indicates to me that we are up against something very profound, very stubborn, something we cannot root out simply by rearranging a few tasks and roles in the social system, or even by reordering the whole economic structure.[134]

Although it is a feminist scholar who writes thus, what have feminists and their sympathizers done? Rearranged tasks and roles in the social system. They have made "Mr. Mom" a familiar concept. They have popularized female construction workers, cops, and firemen. They have forced the admittance of women into all male clubs and societies. And even though Ortner concluded that female subordination cannot be addressed or redressed by a reordering of our economic structure, what has happened? Feminists have all but reordered our entire economic system by driving women into the workforce, removing the "glass ceiling" so that women could be over men, and insisting that women needed affirmative action programs to be fair.

Gender polarity is a fact of our society because it is a fact of our creation. The fact that some feminists see that male-female roles and relationships are much deeper, more profound, and more stubborn than circumstances, custom, or tradition could create, shows that even they, if only faintly, see something beyond humanity in them; they, too, see something of the divine in the male-female polarity. In other words, they see a religious connection, thereby warning those of the True Religion that we had better be very careful about tinkering with this polarity, and we had better "man" the battle stations against all attackers and compromisers.

Yes, when we deal with the male-female polarity in

creation, we are dealing not only in the domain of sociology but theology; not only with science but religion; not just with the bodies of men and women but with souls. The feminists alerted us to this fact when Betty Friedan told us that the women's movement was "almost a religious experience"[135] for her and that what the feminist movement hoped to accomplish was theological in nature.[136]

We in the Church should have realized that feminism was interfering with things of a divine nature when so many feminists refused to admit that they were doing so and insisted they were only dealing with the things of men. Consider the following examples: feminist Nancy Cott said in 1987, "If women's condition were entirely determined by its natural or divine origins, then there would be no possibility for change."[137] Feminist Mary Daly said that if your view was that God was done revealing His will at the end of the Apostolic age, then "certain statements in the Bible represent descriptions of an unalterable divine plan..."[138] And nineteenth century feminist Margaret Fuller said she would indeed be silent for a hundred years, "if that silence be from divine command and not from man's traditions."[139]

But feminists know that we are talking about a divine not a human matter when it comes to the distinction between masculine and feminine. However, they are convinced that God is a feminist. This is the only conviction feminists with consciences can have since they would find themselves opposing God if God is not a feminist. But if God is not a feminist, then feminism is in opposition to the true God, and so is every condescension, compromise, or surrender to feminism. The feminists know that if God is a feminist, then their crusade is religious in nature and they dare not give it up. Why is it then, that those who do not believe God is a feminist have given up the crusade against it? Have not the feminists taught us at least this much: that there is no third position between feminism and Christianity, regardless of whether such positions are called Christian feminism or feminized Christianity?

Before leaving this chapter, we want to take a last look at how far feminism has already taken us. The speed and the direction of the descent are warnings to us in themselves. Hopefully they will move us to deeper study of this phenomenon that is not merely social or historical, but above all else theological.

As a society, as a church, and even as individuals we have marched boldly forward ever deeper into feminism despite what has happened so far. Almost any non-feminist who stands back and looks with a critical eye upon the affect feminism has had on society would have to conclude that it has been injurious. Writing in 1980, Stephen Clark noted six destructive trends of feminism: 1) family life is weakened; 2) sexual relationships become troubled; 3) women often lose a sense of value; 4) womanly roles are neglected or institutionalized; 5) manly roles are neglected—men lose the ability to approach their roles in a characteristically male way; 6) men and women develop psychological instabilities.[170] The *trends* Clark identified over fifteen years ago are the *patterns* of today's society; they are what everyone from talk show hosts to politicians bemoan. Yet we continue down the path of feminism. Why is such a destructive force so incredibly hard to resist?

It must be hard to resist, since we continue to surrender. We continue down a path that even the feminists warned us is lined with pain! In 1978 feminist journalist Barbara Seaman wrote this bleak description of where feminism took her:

> I was in an early-consciousness-raising group, which proved effective. We all went on to publish books, get Phds, or rise up some way in the world. Years later, those of us who were mothers tried to reassemble in order to measure the price our families might have paid. The sessions were so painful that after five or six of them we quit. Too many husbands had deserted

(one for a playboy bunny), too many children had dropped out of school, turned gay, attempted suicide. To a man the divorced husbands, however affluent, were copping out on child support, college tuitions and psychiatrist bills.[141]

When feminists themselves look at the results, they know something is wrong. They have met their goal of 'uplifting' women, but they seem to have trampled men, marriage, and family in the process. If Christians continue down the path of feminism, we will do the same thing, and we will see in the Church what Betty Friedan noted in society twenty years after writing *The Feminist Mystique*:

I go into a town to lecture, and I hear about all the wonderful, dynamic women who have emerged in every field in that town. But frequently, whatever the age of the woman, she says, "There don't seem to be any men. The men seem so dull and gray now. They're dreary, they're flat, they complain, they're tired."[142]

It was noted that the more active and vocal women are in a group the more passive and quiet the men are. Most men are quite content (sinfully so) to have their wives as active as they want to be as long as they can be passive and not re-sponsible. But as the quote from Friedan shows, they cease to be masculine.

Feminism has robbed us of our men and of our women by its persistent war against the masculine-feminine polarity. But a casuality of this combat is the concern of men for women. As late as 1969, as least 26 states had laws categorically barring women from holding certain jobs on the grounds of protecting them.[143] Such thinking today is labeled sexist, patronizing or worse. In today's world, if you want to be considered as really being "for women," you have to want to see them grimy and dirty on construction jobs, wrestling with drunks two times their size as police officers, and crawling through war zones as infantry soldiers.

But before a man will accept (let alone advocate) this, he will have to have had his respect for women turned down or off. The Israelis proved this already in 1948. At that time a handful of women saw combat with the Jewish defense forces. The presence of women on the battlefield led to higher casualties. "Israeli men risked their lives and missions to protect their women, and Arab troops fought more fiercely to avoid the humiliation of being defeated by women. The women were withdrawn after three weeks."[144]

After the 1991 Gulf War as a chaplain for a Graves Registration unit that was mobilized, the author read a report on Mortuary Affairs Operations in the theater. In postwar interviews soldiers reported that what bothered them the most about processing casualties was dealing with the remains of women and children. This is how it should be; it is part of the male-female polarity that the Lord has implanted in us. Men should not want to see women as dirty, smelly, and traumatized as they are. But if women are going to be "fully integrated" into society, this is what must happen. The military asserts that in order for women to be used successfully on the battlefield men must overcome, "their natural impulses to treat women differently and more considerately."[145]

We are long way down this particular path of feminism already. When the U.S. Senate made its original inquiry into the sinking of the *Titanic*, an officer from the ship was asked why they discriminated and got the women and children off first. A senator, trying to be helpful said, "Why did you do that? Because of the Captain's orders or because of the rule of the sea?" The ship's officer replied simply, "The rule of human nature."[146] Human nature has not fared so well since then. The Pittsburgh *Post-Gazette* did a survey in 1992, eighty years after the sinking of the *Titanic*. It found that only 35 percent of the men would give way to women and children.[147]

In fact, feminists have come so far as to turn on babies. This does not shock us anymore 25 years after *Roe v. Wade*, but it would have shocked the nineteenth century feminists. Even the most radical feminists of that time, "excoriated contraception—as well as abortion—as sinful and harmful."[148] Even in the early twentieth century a radical feminist and anarchist like Emma Goldman could write, "Fortunately, the most rigid Puritans never will be strong enough to kill the innate craving for motherhood."[149]

A Puritanical view of sexuality did not kill the craving for motherhood; feminism did. Feminism championed the right of mothers to kill their babies at will. Feminism has replaced the barbaric Roman *patriae potestas* where a Roman father could kill any member of his family without punishment with an equally barbaric "*matriae*" *potestas* where an American mother can kill her unborn baby anytime she wants to without punishment. In those who use or defend this "right," the "innate craving for motherhood" has effectively been killed.

So feminism has led to men giving up their special regard for women and to women giving up their special regard for children. Men are not concerned with being able to (or even trying to) provide for women, and women are not concerned with taking care of children. The individual, whether male or female, reigns supreme. A male will seek to provide for a female when it fits into his plans, and a female will care for a child when it fits into hers. But this is not how God originally ordered things. For families and societies to function, males have to be concerned for females and females for children even when it is not convenient. But what we have now is not a society, not a community, but a tyranny of individualism where nothing rules but self.

This is how pagan males have always lived; now pagan females have it that way, too. One sees this throughout the history of feminism: Whatever fallen men have, in their baseness, women want too, but they inevitably want to take it one step further.

August Bebel, a socialist and a feminist of the early 1900s, said that a woman's education should be the same as a man's. She did, however, allow for deviations based on the differences of sex and sexual functions.[150] Women achieved this goal from the '20s onward, but this was not enough. When the second wave of feminism washed over colleges in the '60s and '70s, feminists were not content on being educated in the same way as men. They wanted courses even more self-centered than the male ones. And so now women have courses such as, "Lesbian Studies: Creating Choices Both Inside and Outside the University," "Female Deities: Historical Perspectives," "On the Barricades for Abortion Rights," and "Lesbian Mothering." Feminism always goes to the extreme, one step beyond what even the most self-centered of males would do. For example, at the 1992 National Women's Studies Association conference in Austin, Texas, two films were offered in the evening, "Sex and the Sandinistas" and "We're Talking Vulva."[151]

Once we fall away from the "magnetic" pull of the male-female polarity, we fall farther and farther away from not only Christianity, but reason and common sense. Mary Pride, an ex-feminist, comments, "We are being asked to embrace a lifestyle which unbelievers would have considered perverted only forty years ago!"[152]

She is right, but the effects of feminism are not only felt in their perversity. Feminism has subtly turned institutions away from their God-given purposes. Many can see how it has done this to marriage and family, and many are afraid of what it is doing to the Church. But not many have noticed what is has already done to the third basic divine institution in society: the state or government. It is here that feminism has had some of its most far reaching effects, and this, in turn, has helped it get its tentacles more tightly around the family and the Church.

What feminism has done to government is not what those opposed to woman suffrage said would happen. Women did not end up voting as a gigantic block. Neither did they end up running the government. What they did end up doing is far more serious; they ended up feminizing it. Jane Addams observed already in 1907, "Most of the departments in a modern city can be traced to woman's traditional activity..."[153] Contrast this with the Scriptural understanding of government as doing basically masculine tasks: bearing the sword, hindering and punishing lawbreakers, providing for the common defense.

Make no mistakes about it; feminization is exactly what the feminists believed the government needed. When those opposed to suffrage said that giving women the vote would take them into politics and away from charity, one feminist replied, "Thank God, there will not be so much need of charity and philanthropy."[154] This woman was almost prophetic because the welfare state has most certainly usurped the place of charities and benevolence.

However, this is not the purpose for which God created government, and this is not what government was until women got the vote in 1920. The very first allocation of federal funds for a welfare program took place in 1921 at the instigation of the Women's Joint Congressional Committee. This committee saw to the Sheppard-Towner Act becoming law. (It was also known as the Maternity and Infancy Act.)

Women got into the halls of government and insisted that government take care of people like an all-powerful mother not realizing that this is where the 1984 concept of "Big Brother" comes from. Women insisted that there would not be as many wars if they were in government. They demanded a kinder, gentler government, and they got it. The punishment of the death penalty gave way to the concept of rehabilitation. The welfare state ballooned to take care of everyone during some portion of their life and some people all of their lives. And there were fewer declared wars. A feminized people would not tolerate them; instead we had "conflicts" called Korea and Vietnam. We have "police actions" and "military operations" to "shield" the innocent, rather than wars to defeat the vicious. And we have come to use our military for humane, almost feminine, pursuits like building roads in South America, feeding the starving in Somalia, and mentoring troubled youth in American schools.

A shift has taken place, and we have all been caught up in it. The male-female polarity which used to permeate all of society has constantly been denied, attacked, and short-circuited. Where everything used to be ordered male-female according to the divinely-ordained masculine-feminine polarity, now everything is ordered by group consensus, scientific efficiency, psychological models, or personal preferences. No one is sure what men or women are suppose to do, so everyone tries to behave as a 'person'. But people are either male or female, and if they cease to behave as either masculine or feminine, then in some real, tangible sense, they cease to behave as people and they become more like animals.

Why have we let feminism take us, sometime very willingly, so far away from the God-given polarity we all know we need? Why is feminism so hard to resist?

Notes:

1   Will & Ariel Durant, *The Age of Voltaire*, (New York: MJF Books, 1965) 156.
2   ibid., 116-117.
3   ibid., 781.
4   Betty Friedan, *The Feminine Mystique*, (New York: Dell Publishing, 1983) 103-104.
5   Friedan, 123.
6   Nancy F. Cott, *The Grounding of Feminism*, (New Haven: Yale University Press, 1987) 19-20.
7   Christina Hoff Sommers, *Who Stole Feminism?*, (New York: Simon & Schuster, 1994) 21-22.
8   Carl N. Degler, *At Odds*, (New York: Oxford University Press, 1980) 326.
9   Cott, 48-49.
10   Harvey Green, *The Light of the Home*, (New York: Panethon Books, 1983) 98.

[11] Green, 21-22.

[12] Alexis de Tocqueville, *Democracy in America*, vol. 2, trans. Henry Reeve, (New York: Vintage Books, 1990) 211.

[13] Stephen B. Clark, *Man and Woman in Christ*, (Ann Arbor: Servant Books, 1980) 654.

[14] Degler, 181.

[15] Clark, 296.

[16] Degler, 306.

[17] Freidan, 92.

[18] Green, 149.

[19] Degler, 302.

[20] Mary A. Kassian, *The Feminist Gospel*, (Wheaton: Crossway Books, 1992) 172.

[21] Friedan, 98.

[22] *The Age of Voltaire*, 598.

[23] Degler, 299.

[24] Ann Douglas, *The Feminization of American Culture*, (New York: Alfred A. Knopf, 1977) 207.

[25] Clarence B. Carson, *A Basic History of the United States*, vol. 3, The Sections and the Civil War 1826-1877, (Wadley, AL: American Textbook Committee, 1985) 82-83.

[26] Cott, 3.

[27] *The Feminist Papers*, ed. by Alice S. Rossi, (Boston: Northeastern University Press, 1973) xiii.

[28] Cott, 3.

[29] ibid., 36.

[30] *Feminist Papers*, 414.

[31] Degler, 346.

[32] ibid., 347.

[33] ibid., 346.

[34] ibid., 446.

[35] Cott, 226.

[36] Degler, 416.

[37] ibid., 420.

[38] ibid., 422.

[39] ibid., 439.

[40] ibid., 424.

[41] Friedan, 8.

[42] Degler, 442.

[43] ibid., 444.

[44] Friedan, 388.

[45] *Feminist Papers*, xxiv.

[46] Marilee Horton, *Free To Stay at Home*, (Waco: Word Publishing, 1982) 85.

47 John Pollock, *The Apostle*, (Wheaton: Victor Books, 1972) 87.
48 Gregory L. Jackson, *Liberalism: Its Cause and Cure*, (Milwaukee: Northwestern, 1991) 84.
49 Clark, 303.
50 The Ante-Nicene Fathers, vol. 1, 316.
51 Ante-Nicene Fathers, vol. 1, 317, n.4.
52 Deborah Belonick, *Feminism in Christianity (An Orthodox Christian Response)*, (Syosset, New York: Department of Religious Education, Orthodox Church in America, 1983) 105.
53 Clark, 307
54 The Ante-Nicene Fathers, vol. VII, eds. Alexander Roberts and James Donaldson, (Grand Rapids: Eerdmans, 1985) 427-428.
55 Ante-Nicene Fathers, VII, 429.
56 Martin Luther, *Luther's Works*, ed. Jaroslav Pelikan, vol. 12, "Selections From the Psalms," trans. L.W. Spitz, Jr., (St. Louis: Concordia, 1955) 48.
57 Martin Chemnitz, *The Lord's Supper*, trans. J.A.O. Preus, (St. Louis: Concordia, 1979) 268.
58 W.H.T. Dau, "Prefatory Note," Woman Suffrage in the Church, *Moving Frontiers*, ed. Carl S. Meyer, (St. Louis: Concordia, 1964) 380.
59 Clark, 248-249.
60 ibid., 251.
61 ibid., 254.
62 ibid., 317.
63 Elisabeth Elliot, The Mark of a Man, (Grand Rapids: Fleming H. Revell, 1981) 29.
64 Bacchiocchi, *Women in the Church*, (Berrien Springs: Biblical Perspectives, 1987) 98.
65 ibid., 146-147.
66 Kurt Marquart, *The Church*, vol. IX, Confessional Lutheran Dogmatics, Robert Preus, ed., (Ft. Wayne: The International Foundation for Lutheran Confessional Research, 1990) 166.
67 Steichen, *Ungodly Rage*, (San Francisco: Ignatius Press, 1991) 40.
68 ibid., 27.
69 Kassian, 144.
70 ibid., 185.
71 ibid., 224.
72 Alan Morrison, *The Serpent and the Cross*, (Birmingham: K&M Books, 1994) 305-306.
73 ibid., 316.
74 Cott, 248.
75 ibid., 137.
76 Clark, 586.
77 David J. Ayers, "The Inevitability of Failure: The Assumptions and Implemen-

tations of Modern Feminism", *Recovering*, 315.

[78] John Leo, *U.S. News & World Report*, August 11, 1997, 14.

[79] Clark, 637.

[80] Douglas, 76.

[81] Degler, 447.

[82] Gilder, 138.

[83] Degler, 392.

[84] ibid., 315.

[85] Brian Mitchell, *Weak Link*, (Washington, D.C.: Regenery Gateway, 1989) 225.

[86] Sommers, 267-268.

[87] Steven Goldberg, *Why Men Rule*, (Chicago: Open Court, 1993) 115.

[88] ibid., 115.

[89] Degler, 48.

[90] ibid., 48.

[91] ibid., 49.

[92] *Feminist Papers*, 205.

[93] Friedan, 181.

[94] Clark, 421.

[95] Gilder, 132.

[96] Goldberg, 14.

[97] ibid., 15.

[98] ibid., 30.

[99] ibid., 52.

[100] Clark, 417.

[101] Goldberg, 45.

[102] ibid., 35.

[103] ibid., 41.

[104] Iliad, vi.

[105] Goldberg, 23.

[106] Mitchell, 204.

[107] Robert N. Bellah, et al., *Habits of the Heart*, (New York: Harper & Row, 1985) 111.

[108] Gilder, *Men and Marriage*, (Gretna: Pelican Publishing Company, 1986) 43.

[109] Will and Ariel Durant, *Rousseau and Revolution*, (New York: MJF Books, 1967) 186.

[110] Gilder, 122.

[111] Roger Welsch, "Song for a Pioneer", *Audubon*, (Nov.-Dec. '92).

[112] Friedan, 86.

[113] Rossi, Feminist Papers, 86-97.

[114] Degler, 276.

[115] "To Manipulate Woman", Concerned Women for America Tract, no date.

[116] Rossi, 37.

[117] Rossi, 37.

[118] Cott, 13.

[119] ibid.

[120] ibid., 61.

[121] F. Carolyn Graglia, "The Breaking of the "Women's Pact"", *The Weekly Standard*, Nov. 11, 1996, pp.29-33.

[122] Degler, 360.

[123] ibid., 402.

[124] Cott, 138.

[125] ibid., 128-129.

[126] ibid., 198.

[127] *The Feminist Papers*, 84, 52.

[128] ibid., 514.

[129] Friedan, 142.

[130] ibid., 86.

[131] *The Feminist Papers*, 200.

[132] Cott, 199.

[133] *The Feminist Papers*, 678.

[134] Clark, 414, 423.

[135] Friedan, 398.

[136] Steichen, 29.

[137] Cott, 5.

[138] Kassian, 41.

[139] *The Feminist Papers*, 174.

[140] Clark, 442-443.

[141] Clark, 444.

[142] Friedan, xxii-xxiii.

[143] Degler, 404.

[144] Mitchell, 205.

[145] Gilder, 136.

[146] William Oddie, *What Will Happen To God?*, (San Francisco: Ignatius Press, 1988) 32.

[147] Time, April 27, 1992.

[148] Degler, 198.

[149] *The Feminist Papers*, 512.

[150] ibid., 502.

[151] Sommers, 32.

[152] Pride, 11.

[153] *The Feminist Papers*, 607-608.

[154] Cott, 100.

CHAPTER II
FEMINISM APPEALS TO THE
SPIRIT OF THE AGE

In this matter of feminism, we certainly are not wrestling against flesh and blood (whether male or female) but against the spirit of this age which is always at work among the sons of disobedience and the daughters of men. Feminism is not really about redressing the very real wrongs that men have done and still do to women. It is not about fairness. It is not about women "finally getting the recognition they deserve." What feminism is about is undoing God's created order.

Like all movements, causes, or thoughts that have their origins in hell, feminism is stamped with the telling signs of Satan. He always works in a way which is the opposite of the way in which God works. God's basic unit in society is the home. God works though the home to the Church and out into the world. Satan's basic unit is the mob. He works through the mob-led world to the Church and into the home. Like Martin Luther, Satan realizes that in the end the last vestiges of Christianity will be preserved by godly fathers in their homes. If the home, the foundation of society, is destroyed, what are the righteous to do about it?

Feminism originates in the world, and, as such, appeals to the spirit of the age. The best label for the spirit of this present age is "American." In fact, feminism is the full flowering of American ideals, principles, and values. Succinctly put: it is UN-American *not* to be a feminist. America drinks up feminism even as she has swallowed up almost every other cause that appeals to its 'trinity' of liberty, equality, and justice for individuals.

The fact that feminism is so palatable to Americans should have been a plus for the Church. Here, for once, Christians could see a clear parting of the ways between Christianity and America. Here, for once, Christians could see that "American" does *not* equal "Christian." Here, as prophesied in the Book of Revelation, the earth was serving the Church by opening her mouth wide to swallow the flood of delusion that spewed from Satan's mouth in an attempt to carry the Church away (Revelation 12: 15,16).

But there was a problem and it was not a new one. The Church had experienced it before when Christianity was legalized in the early fourth century. At that time people poured into the Church bringing the world with them. "Later Christians gradually lost a consciousness of the Scriptural meaning of opposition to the world as all members of society gradually became members of the Christian church."[1] Feminism feels so right to so many in the Church because they are at home in the world. Rather than the Church turning the world upside down as she moves out into it, the world is turning the Church upside down as it moves into her. Feminism *feels* so right, so American!

Principles, ideals, and values that we have come to think of as American, and in many cases even as Christian, flow from the same headwaters as feminism. These headwaters are the eighteenth century Enlightenment. Secular sociologist Steven Goldberg says that eighteenth century feminists, "grounded their feminist demands on Enlightenment principles of individual justice."[2] Feminist authority Nancy Cott shows that Enlightenment principles flowed into the nineteenth century woman movement and out into the twentieth century women's rights movement. "The tradition that most obviously nourished woman's rights advocates was Enlightenment rationalism, its nineteenth-century political legacy liberalism, and its social representation bourgeois individualism."[3]

In the first chapter, it was observed that something went radically wrong in Victoria's era (i.e., the nineteenth century). Having cast off Biblical authority in the eighteenth century, nineteenth century America (which lacked history or tradition to keep things in check), in particular, spewed forth an amazing cesspool of ideas. Although ideas such as communism, socialism, new age (then called spiritism), feminism, revolution, and evolution did not originate in America, they took root, blossomed, and produced fruit here as nowhere else. In the words of one living at the time, Dr. Henry Gibson (a former head of the California Medical Society), "Our age and our country, alive with free and busy thought, have given birth to a number of abnormalities, if not monstrosities, religious, intellectual, and moral."[4] He made this comment from the vantage point of 1877.

Feminism enjoys a broad base of support outside of the Church and beyond typical God, mother, and apple pie American culture because it is linked with other lies of this age that issued forth from Satan's mouth. The standard feminist agenda today is abortion, homosexuality, 'spirituality', and revolutionary politics.[5] One can well understand why abortion would be on the feminist agenda, but why the others? Because they are all 'in sync' with the spirit of this age; they are, in fact, siblings.

Francis Schaeffer, in his book *The Great Evangelical Disaster*, shows not only how abortion is linked to feminism, but also how homosexuality is linked to it. Moreover, he makes the philosophical case for seeing homosexuality as growing directly out of feminism. Perhaps more startling still, he opines that abortion stems from homosexuality—not feminism, as most often surmised:

> If we accept the idea of equality without distinctions, we logically must accept the idea of abortion and homosexuality. For if there are no significant distinctions between men and women, then certainly we cannot condemn homosexual relationships....This fiction can be maintained only by the use of abortion on demand

as a means of coping with the most profound evidence that distinctions really do exist.[6]

Schaeffer saw a link between feminism, homosexuality, and abortion. There is also a link between feminism, new age spirituality, and revolutionary politics. Tenets of new age spirituality are: despair with present society, search for enlightenment within, and a vision of transformed global order.[7] See how this matches up with present day feminist thinkers in the Roman Catholic Church. Sister Madonna Kolbenschlag says, "Woman's spirituality....is building a kind of chrysalis of the future" out of which she expects the new world order to emerge.[8] Rosemary Ruether says, "A new God is being born in our hearts....to teach us to level the heavens and exalt the earth and create a new world order."[9]

Feminist spirituality will serve revolutionary politics even as revolutionary politics has already served the cause of feminism. When Liberation theology was on the cutting edge in the late 1970s, Rosemary Reuther was already identifying feminist theology as a species of the popular and very political Liberation theology.[10]

Feminism has common cause not only with 1970s revolutionary Liberation theology but with nineteenth century communism and socialism. Although not biased against feminism, sociologist Goldberg concludes that the classical assumptions of feminism about how societies evolve (i.e., matrilineality precedes and must precede patrilineality; matrilineality is transformed to patrilineality by the advent of private property and class differentiation; early stages of societal development are not merely matrilineal but matriarchal) are based on the works of Friedrich Engels, the co-author of *The Communist Manifesto.*[11]

Those in our age who are of a communist-Marxist bent will resonate to the drum beats of feminism. The communist's call to eliminate class privilege corresponds to the feminist's call to eliminate what it regards as male privilege. And the former's call to eliminate class distinctions corresponds to the latter's call to eliminate sex distinctions.

Those in our age who lean toward socialism will find fellow travelers within feminism. Feminist August Bebel (1840-1913) proclaimed as much in 1902: "Those who seek a complete solution of the women question must, therefore, join hands with those who have inscribed upon their banner the solution of the social question in the interest of all mankind—the socialists."[12]

In the first chapter, we saw that the first instance of government money being used for a welfare program was spearheaded by women immediately after women got the vote. Also in January 1921, the League of Women Voters had in their platform the following, heretofore considered socialist, planks: federal aid to education, old-age insurance, and unemployment insurance.[13] At present, such one-time socialist causes are as American as baseball.

A popular modern-day plank in the feminist platform is "comparable worth." Who could be opposed to this? What red-blooded American worker does not think equal pay for comparable work is a good concept? But this is, as it has been called, "the feminist road to socialism." The problem is in defining what a job is worth objectively across the board. What employers will pay a man or woman for a particular job is based on what the market will bear, and they pay it to those employees who prove their worth to them at doing the job. Feminists would have the government subjectively, by fiat, declare that jobs typically done by females are worth as much as some jobs typically done by males and that a woman doing the same job as a man does it exactly to the same standard. This is socialism.[14]

Socialism, communism, a new world order—these movements are not all that 'revolutionary' anymore. Radical environmentalism still has a 'revolutionary' image, yet this, too, will find much to like in feminism. Feminist Rosemary Reuther says that feminists cannot criticize the hierarchy of man over woman, "without ultimately criticizing the hierarchy of humans over nature."[15]

The spirit found in feminism can be linked to the spirits found in many (if not most) of the present day opponents of God's created order, and these spirits have coalesced in one place—America. The spirit of this present age can be summed up by one word—American! As nationalities once sought our land, our natural resources, and our freedom, today's nations want our culture, our values. They want liberty, equality, and justice for the individual and a democratic political system for the nation. In America's early history, liberty, equality, and justice for the individual were generally not sought, and they were certainly not granted at the expense of the society. That has changed; now they are. This is the intoxicating spirit of the age that so many seek, and it fits 'hand in glove' with feminism. The ideology of feminism is the ideology of America.

Feminists past and present testify to this. In the 1920s, feminist Beatrice Forbes Robertson Hale attributed the feminist revolution to, "the inevitable effect of two forces: the theory of democracy and the fact of industrialism."[16] Writing in 1994, feminist Christina Hoff Sommers (although herself against feminist excesses) concludes, "Credos and intellectual fashions come and go but feminism itself—the pure and wholesome article first displayed at Seneca Falls in 1848—is as American as apple pie, and it will stay."[17]

Feminism and America share a common ideology. This is important to realize because ideologies appeal to a person's conscience. When an ideology is rejected, guilt will be felt unless an alternate ideology or moral rebuttal is set against it.[18] What alternate ideology or moral rebuttal do American Christians have to democracy? What response can they give to neo-pagan ideologies that come to them wrapped in the same flag that they see in their chancels every Sunday? Why is feminism so hard to resist? Because it fits in with everything Americans have been raised to believe in and revere: liberty, equality, justice, individualism, and the workings of democratic politics.

For example, what patriotic American can resist an appeal to liberty of action, an appeal to their "rights?" The Declaration of Independence from a king's rule, the Constitution which forms a government which protects the liberty of individuals, and, of course, the Bill of Rights are sacred, hallowed, cherished documents to most Americans. The Freemen, a militia group in Montana who were under siege by the FBI for criminal violations in May 1996, were reported to be actually worshipping the Constitution as an idol.

The cry of feminism has been historically, "We have rights! We are as free as men! We must be liberated!" Feminism is only echoing the cry of fallen man. Sinful men have always asserted their rights. In the eighteenth century, they asserted their right to be free of biblical authority. In the latter part of that same century, they asserted their right to have their world free of kings and churches. The nineteenth century saw them assert their right to be an individual. But it was left to our century, the twentieth, to see what sinful men would become once they were cut loose from God and earthly authority, being finally at liberty to do and be anything they wanted to be.

Feminist leaders saw the path men took and they wanted to go down it, too. They wanted to be FREE. They had as much a RIGHT to that as the men did. A 1969 feminist poster put it this way: "This time we will be free or no one will survive."[19] Women are now much more 'free' than in 1969, but an incredible number of people did not survive the struggle. About 1.5 million American babies a year are not surviving life in the womb, and this is a consequence of women gaining the same freedom as sinful men. Sinful men have no other allegiance than to self; why should not the same be true for sinful women? If men have no responsibility to have children and every right to walk away from them, why should women not have this same right?

Liberty for women is inextricably linked to abortion. A woman's right to liberty must include the right to kill her unborn baby or she will never be as free as a man. In fact, this one 'right' will be her most "sacred and important right" without which she cannot be truly liberated. That is what an 1858 spiritists' free convention concluded when they passed this resolution:

> 6. That the most sacred and important right of woman, is her right to decide for herself how often and under what circumstances she shall assume the responsibilities and be subject to the cares and suffering of maternity...[20]

In 1858 feminist thinkers had to dance around the sensitive issue of abortion, but they could be much bolder by 1914. In that year, an article in a feminist magazine said, "If a woman is to free herself effectively, she must make herself absolute mistress of her own body. She must recognize her absolute right...to suppress the germ of life."[21] And see how the founder of Planned Parenthood, Margaret Sanger, buries the right of abortion in the *credo* of her magazine, *The Woman Rebel*, in the April 1914 issue:

> The Rebel Women Claim:
> The Right to be Lazy.
> The Right to be an unmarried mother.
> The Right to destroy.
> The Right to create.
> The Right to love.
> The Right to live.[22]

"And ye shall be as gods!" That is what Satan promised, and that is what Sanger's creed asserts. Still, talk of 'liberty' and 'rights' strikes a deep (if base) chord in our American hearts.

A second, hallowed spirit of the age of democracy is equality. Equality, even more than liberty, has served the cause of feminism. As one writer has put it, "Feminism owes really all of its success to the western world's unqualified enthusiasm for an ill-defined doctrine of equality."[23] In the realm of the physical, things cannot be made equal except by the application of some type of force. Two pieces of lumber are made equal by the force of the saw blade. Mountains are made equal in height by the force of dynamite. Clay sculptures are made equal by adding to or by taking away from one or the other. Equality in the physical realm only comes by the use of force; this axiom is true in the realm of people too.

There are differences *between* the sexes and even within the sexes. Some sort of force needs to be applied to make equality where God did not make it. A Texas proverb from the days of the Old West illustrates this well: "God made some men big and some men small, but Sam Colt made them all equal." The Colt pistol was the great equalizer of the Old West. The invention of a mass market pistol made it so that physical size and/or strength no longer determined who won fights or ruled towns.

Equality is a cherished, sacred American principle, but originally it was equality of *opportunity*; everyone in America had the equal opportunity to be all they could be within the limits of their God-given abilities. However, since the 1960s equality of *opportunity* has come to be thought of as equality of *result*; everyone should be able to be all that anyone else is, regardless of their abilities.

But equality of result can only be achieved by force and with a corresponding loss of liberty. Alexander Hamilton, one of America's founding fathers, recognized this. He said, "Inequality will exist as long as liberty exists. It unavoidably results from that very liberty itself." Or in the words of a modern commentator on Hamilton's words, "Free men are not equal and equal men are not free."[24]

More than liberty is at stake, however: our understanding of God is, too. God reveals Himself through contrast (Law-Gospel) and inequalities (wrath-mercy). In fact, God begins His self-revelation in Genesis with a startling list of opposites: heavens/earth; light/darkness; firmament/waters; land/sea; sun/moon; planets/stars; plants/animals; male/female. As you follow this list, words such as "equal," "same," and "interchangeable" do not come to mind. Words like "inequality," "different," and "distinction" do.[25] When we see the male/female polarity revealing, in some sense, the image of God, then the idea of equality is out of place because if male and female are equal, then they do not each convey in their own distinct way something about God—only "humanity" does, not masculinity and femininity.[26]

Equality is a principle run amuck in America. The uncritical acceptance of this principle has legitimized the feminist cry of "equality, equality!" in the midst of where there is none. Even feminists must know this deep down. MS. magazine has an executive editor, and the National Organization for Women has a president.[27] You can bet that no one in these organizations thinks of passing such positions around the feminist camp as if they were all equal and it didn't matter which one of them was the executive editor or president.

But if one advocates any other organization be operated based on the principle that God created men and women different from one another, not equal, not interchangeable, feminists would label him sexist, prejudiced, and downright un-American. If one sees value in role differences for men and women, he will be charged with under-valuing women.[28] Unless one agrees to the principle of role interchangeability, he will be charged with denying equality of worth.[29] Unless one agrees that boys and girls should be dressed, treated, and disciplined in the same way, unless one gets dolls for his boys and trucks for his girls, he will be charged with denying equality, although all he is really doing is recognizing differences and distinctions that nearly everyone recognized up until the 1960s.[30]

Equality of worth is God-given; equality of result, task, or role must be forced. For example, since the majority of high school valedictorians are female, one could insist that an equal number be males. Likewise, one could insist that there be an equal number of males in the Miss America pageant. One could further insist—for the sake of equality—that it be legislated that one male and one female must win. In order that equality might reign—that is, *rule*—one could insist that formal "sweet-sixteen" balls in New Orleans be held for males, too.

How absurd such things would be! Force would be called on to create an equality that did not freely exist. But this is what the feminists have done. Our present day military is a good example: to make it *appear* that men and women are equal in physical ability, physical fitness test scorers are forced to use two different standards—one for men and one for women. The same amount of pushups and sit-ups, the same time in the run counts *more* for women than it does for men. Scores from these physical fitness tests are used to determine who gets promoted, who gets school slots, who gets awards, but they have been artificially weighted in favor of women since the early 1980s.

Feminists could not get away with such manipulating to create the illusion of equality where there is none if equality were not such a shibboleth of our age. But equality of "sex" became a shibboleth almost by accident. It was pointed out in the first chapter that "sex" was added to the Civil Rights Act of 1964 by a Southern congressman hoping to derail its passage. To his surprise, President Johnson came out in favor of the addition and eventually signed it into law. That addition had the effect of making "Help Wanted Male," "Help Wanted Female" signs as illegal as "Help Wanted Colored."[31]

Once the law was passed, feminism cheered and the spirit of this age was lined up squarely against the truth. Now appealing to role distinctions or just pointing out differences between men and women is a moral failure, a prejudice, a civil rights violation. In the American understanding of things, you become a sinner if you assert the God-given distinctiveness of male and female and advocate that home, church, and society should be ordered that way.

A third icon of our age is justice. Does it *seem* just that the husband should be the head of the home and that a wife should submit to him just because he is male and she is female? Does it seem *just* that a society about to step into the twenty-first century should be guided by a book written in the first? Appeals to 'justice' have great force in our age. Every child who has ever cried to parent or teacher, "But that's not fair!" has learned the principle well and instinctively appeals to a spirit of this age called justice.

Often when a child appeals to justice, it is because his or her sense of fairness has been violated. In a sinful world, it certainly could be true that a child has a more accurate sense of fairness than an adult. But sinful man can never have a more accurate, unbiased sense of fairness or justice than God. Whatever God does or decrees is just and fair. "Who are you O man to reply against God," asks St. Paul when discussing the matter of our questioning God about whom He does and does not have mercy upon. Any challenging of God's justice is blasphemy no matter how right it may sound to us.

But long before feminism blossomed, man had problems with the fairness of God and felt justified in questioning His justice. Is God just for punishing all mankind for Adam's sin? Is God just for damning the savage who never has had a chance to hear the Gospel? Was God just for commanding Israel to destroy every man, woman, child and animal in some cities? Was it fair for the Old Testament sign of the covenant to be one that only a male could bear? Was it fair that descendants of Aaron who had crushed testicles or other physical defects could not be priests? Was it just for God not to name countless mothers and daughters who were instrumental for bringing Christ the Promised Seed into the world?

Matters such as these did not seem just to some men, and so men dismissed them as being of human rather than of divine origin; they are treated as if they were products of a particular culture at a particular time. Women, having their sense of justice violated by the different roles and positions assigned to man and woman, came to the same conclusion about such things: "Christianity has incorporated the dominant patriarchal attitude of the culture of its origin."[32] This leads to the decision: 'Such things as patriarchy, headship, and male-only clergy are products of man; therefore, they can be dismissed at will.'

Feminism has always appealed to a human standard of justice. The five volume work *The History of Woman Suffrage* tells us that the first woman's rights convention in Seneca Falls, New York in 1848 came up with eighteen grievances of women because the fathers of the Declaration of Independence had that many. "[A] protracted search was made through statue books, church usages, and the customs of society to find that exact number..."[33] A sense, a "spirit" of justice demanded that if the men had eighteen grievances, then the women should have that many, too.

In the 1880s, women fought hard against the injustice of prevailing marriage laws that said, in effect, "husband and wife are one, and that one the husband..."[34] It did not seem fair that the individual existence of men should be recognized and not that of women. Perhaps, in view of the prevalence of divorce, it was not wise that a woman should forfeit all of her property rights by marrying, but the solution was not to copy the sin of men and make women individuals, too. Note well, however, that the Bible's understanding is *not* that the two become one flesh and that flesh is the man's—the *two* shall become *one*; *they* are no longer *two* but they are *one* in marriage (Matthew 19:6). The woman alone does not cease to exist; they both do.

It has always worked in this way: the feminist sense of justice is violated by what men do sinfully, so they advocate emulating the sinfulness of men. This, by the way, was the Marquis de Sade's way of solving society's double standard in regard to women. He proposed that the solution to giving men the right to unbridled sexual pleasure while denying the same to women was to grant the same to women.[35] Men are not elevated to a higher standard, but women are lowered to that of fallen men.

But the genuine injustices of men against women are not solved by granting women the same sinful rights as men. This can only have the effect of tearing down society, bringing it down to the lowest common denominator. Is this not exactly what happened in the much-vaunted sexual revolution? Women have been the guardians of the chastity of society because of men's woeful weakness in this area. In general, men have always been prone to saying "yes" when the answer should be "no." The sexual revolution, spurred on by the feminists from the earliest days, said it was only fair that women should be able to be as weak, wretched, and sexually promiscuous as men are.

The truth of the matter is that men should never have been allowed to sow their "wild oats" without sanction. It never should have been, and still should not be so among the people of God, that you could be a "good boy" no matter how much you slept around, but you could only be a "good girl" if you did not. The sexual double standard was wrong, but the solution was not to degenerate the definition of a "good girl" to that of a "good boy."

However, this degeneration only seemed fair, just, and right to fallen human logic; eliminating the double standard by lowering the sexual standard women were expected to uphold to the baseness of men fit in perfectly with the spirit of this age. So the appeal to fairness has given today's woman every sinful right that men have exercised.

But the appeal to fairness has opened doors in the other direction, too; it has not only degraded women to the gutter, it has elevated them to the pastoral office. Most churches have opened the pastoral office to women, and it is considered absolutely essential (after all, it is only fair!) to have woman's leadership on committees and boards. The move upward, however, will not stop with the pastoral office and church leadership. Once the divine standard of justice is thrown out and a human one (female *or* male) is substituted, there will be no stopping till the door to heaven is burst asunder and God Himself is thrown out—at least, that is what they will try to do.

Indeed, this is what is happening in Roman Catholicism, according to Roman Catholic journalist Donna Steichen: "The definitive feminist position is not merely that a religion in which some roles are closed to women is essentially evil but that all hierarchy is evil, even the supernatural hierarchy."[36] This conclusion is only logical: if it is not fair that men should be heads, the leaders, the pastors, the responsible ones, then the God who said they should be certainly cannot be considered just, and therefore, He has lost one of His divine attributes and so ceases to be God.

Liberty, equality, justice—these are the values of our age, and feminism abounds with appeals to them. But there is another factor that makes it doubly difficult to resist appeals to this secular 'trinity': individualism. America, the keeper of the spirit of our age, intends liberty, equality, and justice *for the individual*. Modern America sanctions, blesses, and advocates looking out for "number one." One of the greatest "flaws" in our society is to have low self-esteem. One of the greatest "crimes" in our society is to damage the self-love of anyone else. It has not always been this way; the individual has not always reigned supreme in America, not even among men and certainly not among women.

God is not an advocate of individualism; it was He who said, "It is not good that the man should be alone." One of His glories is that, "He sets the solitary in families" (Psalm 68:6). And He taught us while He walked this earth that the only one who really lives is the one who denies self, crucifies self, loses self, not the one who loves, exalts, or esteems self.

We could spend many pages tracing the rise of this philosophy of individualism that is so unscriptural, so unChrist-like—but we will try to be brief. It is important to know from the start that the basic unit of traditional society prior to the nineteenth century was the family, not the individual. No one was encouraged or rewarded for pursuing self-interest. The man had the duty to provide for his family, so he got a job that enabled him to do that; he did not seek one that would "fulfill" him, but one that would provide for his family. Likewise, the woman cared for the home, not because it was uplifting or gratifying work, but for the sake of her family.

Prior to the nineteenth century, traditional society made little or no use of the category "individual" rights for anyone, male or female. Author Stephen Clark explains the rise of this category:

> This concept is an aspect of the shift from a society based on relational groupings to a society based on a mass of individuals....Before the advent of a tech-nological society, men did not have these "individual rights" either; the structure of traditional society made these rights a meaningless category....As technological society developed, the basic pattern of individualiza-tion was applied more slowly to women and children than to men because the family unity was preserved longer than other relational groupings.[37]

How did the nineteenth century express this newly-discovered *right* to be an individual? The vote. "The suffrage was the essence of feminism in that it asserted the individuality of women and assumed and asserted a woman's self-interest."[38] By what stretch of logic, then, could men who claimed the authority to unseat kings and establish governments by their right to vote deny the vote to fellow human beings? If voting was an inalienable individual right, then it had to be a right of the individual woman, too.

But nineteenth century women who were not feminists knew the score. They understood that suffrage threatened the existence of the family.[39] Antisuffragists maintained that the interest of men and women were identical since they were centered on the welfare of the family. The suffragists held that women were individuals and their interests—even in the family—were different from those of men. Furthermore, the individual (not the family) was the basic unit of the state.[40]

Men have always been prone to individualism. God had to convince Adam that he needed a human companion by having him go through all of the animals in the garden to show him that none were suitable. In Mark Twain's tongue-in-cheek *The Diaries of Adam and Eve*, the first entry after the "new creature with long hair" has arrived says in part, "Cloudy today, wind in the east, think we shall have rain... *We*? Where did I get that word?...I remember now—the new creature uses it."[41]

Men learn from women to say "we," and, for the sake of their women and children, they learn to subdue "I." But feminism has taught fallen women to learn from fallen men to say "I." And once women learned to be conscious of themselves as individuals, they began the campaign against the most intrusive invaders of their individualism: babies. First they did it through contraceptives and then by abortion. The pro-abortion group is very wrong when they assert that a baby is part of a woman's body for her to do with as she pleases. It is precisely because the child is not a part of her body that a woman raised on the rights of individuals believes she has the right to get rid of the child.

The rise of individualism (or, more accurately, the infection of women with that philosophy in the nineteenth century) is what led directly to the precipitous decline in the birthrate of the nineteenth century. It was not that the industrial revolution meant that fewer families needed a large number of field hands and so the birthrate declined. It was not that new methods of birth control suddenly became known. What happened was a new justification was discovered for not having children or for having them on your terms. Historian Carl Degler explains,

> In short, women have always had a reason for limiting children that men have not, but that reason could motivate behavior on a large scale only when women became self-conscious about themselves as individuals—that is, when they began to see themselves as separate from their husbands and their families.[42]

The author's mother has always taken pride in being Mrs. Jay R. Harris; she would never dream of hyphenating her maiden name to her married one. While the author is not prepared to say that all people are morally bound to feel as his mother does, something is wrong when our sense of American individualism causes us to be offended by women who give up their identity as individuals for the sake of their families or by women who are content to be known only as "somebody's mother." How self-less, how Christ-like! How can a family really exist unless someone gives up self for the sake of it?

However, the spirit of this age is individualism, so when feminists speak of the "horror" of women losing their individual identity, we sympathize with their cause, probably because we, male and female, have asserted our right to be "me" so many times before. Individualism is the real motive behind young brides demanding the word "submit" or "obey" be stricken from their marriage vows. If she "stands under" (the literal meaning of the Greek word translated "submit" or "obey" in Ephesians 5) her husband, she does indeed lose some of her identity. And he loses some of his when he agrees to be her head for life. The spirit of individualism is shown in the extreme when after the bride and groom light the unity candle, they do not blow out their own individual candles. Such an act flies in the face of the words of Christ found in Matthew 19:6 which words are often read during the marriage service: "The two are no longer two but one."

Marriage, home, and family will not be the only casualties of individualism, so will deity. Feminists will not tolerate a God who in anyway restricts self, so, in effect, what they are left with is the self as god. To show how far this can go, we need only consider the October 1987, "Women in the Church" conference at Cincinnati, Ohio. Three thousand women attended; the majority were nuns and ex-nuns. The main event was the "feminist Eucharist." They consecrated many breads and chalices as representations of the many women present. The consecrated elements became the body and blood of the individual participants.[43]

Of course, this offends any sincere Christian. But cries such as, "I gotta be *me*," "Don't suffocate *me* in marriage," or, "I must pursue what fulfills *me*," strike American ears as only fair, right, and proper even though they are precursors of deifying self. This is because the Siren song sung by the spirit of this age has lulled us to sleep. Our sleepy souls are in danger of shipwreck.

From its American roots at the 1848 Seneca Falls conference, feminism has had its hand on the pulse of the spirit of this age. Feminism has always been very pro-democracy, as can be seen in the list of grievances coming out of the 1848 conference. The list supported the principle of democracy and complained that without the vote women were left without representation.[44] To be disenfranchised is one of the greatest evils in the eyes of the spirit of this age.

A close second is the denial of political power. In America political power, which is obtained through the vote, is everything. One dare not deny political power to groups or individuals. So when feminists argue for political power for women on the basis of their being a group with common interests *and* on the basis of their being individuals in their own right, this is simply an irresistible combination to the average American steeped in the spirit of this age.

On top of arguing that women deserved political power because they are a distinct group and because they are individuals, feminists also argue that the political process *needs* them. It was this argument that ultimately won women the vote. Up until the twentieth century, suffragists argued for the vote by appealing to the fact that women were individuals. This argument failed, so beginning with the twentieth century the suffrage movement talked about the special contributions only women could provide to society based on their characters as wives, mothers, and homemakers.[45] Another historian believes that women succeeded in their cause because opponents were finally convinced that "maternal influence" would halt the dramatic decline of American white, Anglo-Saxon, Protestant culture.[46] Using such lines of reasoning in our day would either earn one the label of sexist or racist.

Recognizing women as *individuals* with something to contribute to the democratic process is in itself no more destructive than recognizing any other individual's distinct gifts and talents. However, something else happens when women are recognized as a separate, distinct group of individuals. Such thinking gives us divided homes, churches, and states. In effect, it makes two *races* out of the one which God created. But once more this is in tune with the spirit of this age which from the multitude of *cultures* that exist has made many *races*. Scriptures, however, only know of one race: the human race. Now that the spirit of this age bestows "racehood" on every distinct culture imaginable, it is unimaginable that this could be denied to female "culture."

However, regarding women as a separate and distinct

culture/race—although assumed by all in the '90s—is something that had to be taught. The teaching took place in the late '60s and early '70s; up till then, the concept was foreign to most people, male or female. Feminist critic Mary Kassian says that it took "incessant exposure" to make a subtle shift in people's minds. People began to view being female as a defining characteristic that cut women out of any other grouping they happened to be in. Then issues such as abortion, pornography, and domestic abuse no longer belonged to society as a whole but were the property and purview of the culture of women.[47] Man is seen as having no political right, and (if it is framed using racial terminology) no moral right, to comment on or to address issues that have been labeled as "women's issues," even though these issues profoundly effect his home, church, and state. Males are regarded as having no more right to comment on "women's issues" than whites do on "black issues." Since the Church was almost exclusively male-led up until 1970, she was effectively cut off from being heard as a relevant commentator on issues that were seen as belonging to the group called women.

Feminism is so hard to resist because it appeals to the hallowed principles of politics that men have lived for, died for, and even deified. But how did feminism succeed in getting women regarded as a separate political unit? First, it had to convince ordinary women that they were and should be—for their own well being—a distinct group. This was done using political tactics invented by fallen men. Kassian explains the process:

> The most effective way to instill in individual women a collective bitterness and unity of purpose was to expose women to other women in the context of small feminist discussion groups. By the process of group dynamics, small sparks of personal unhappiness could be fanned into an inferno of corporate discontent and political action.[48]

This political technique—widely used in the 1970s and now a part of most major university feminist groups—is called "consciousness raising."

"Consciousness raising" comes from the revolutionary army of Mao Tse-tung, which used it in their invasion of North China in the 1940s.[49] (It is still standard practice among Marxists and Communists to use this technique when trying to start a revolt against the established order.) In North China, the process worked as follows: the political revolutionaries wanted to rid villages of Japanese control. They summoned the women of the towns to their town squares, and they had them recite the crimes that men had committed against them. The women were encouraged "to speak bitterness and pain."[50]

"Consciousness raising" is a standard practice of feminists. It is the way feminists get women to think of themselves as individuals distinct from men. As women, they belong to group that is separate from home, church, and state. Instead of seeing relations with men as familial or spiritual in Christ, a woman whose "consciousness" has been "raised" sees her relationship with men as political and as intolerable.

"Consciousness raising" is the way of Satan: first, convince people they have an intolerable situation when they do not, even as Eve was convinced in Paradise itself. Second, convince people that the problem is in others and not in self, even as Adam blamed Eve but not himself. In feminism, the first step divides women from God; the second step divides women from men. Having divided us, Satan conquers. This is what is happening now in our society, in our churches, and even, or probably especially, in our homes. But we are powerless to resist it because it comes to us using political techniques that could sell refrigerators to Eskimos or any cause no matter how morally deficient or spiritually bankrupt it may be.

All of the things in this chapter—liberty, equality, justice, individualism, and politics—are not only hallmarks of our American culture, they are icons of the spirit of this age, and, therefore, they are unchallenged assumptions. However, unless we do challenge them, we will be utterly helpless to resist the assumptions of feminism. The 'mantras' feminism is asking us to chant are the same ones that our American culture has chanted in our ears since birth. The spirit of our age is the spirit of feminism. It is time that we ask, "Are we of the same spirit or not?"

Notes:

[1] Stephen B. Clark, *Man and Woman in Christ*, (Ann Arbor: Servant Books, 1980) 276.

[2] Goldberg, *Why Men Rule*, (Chicago: Open Court, 1993) 22.

[3] Cott, *The Grounding of Feminism*, (New Haven: Yale University Press, 1987) 16.

[4] Marvin Olasky, *Abortion Rites*, (Washington, D.C.: Regnery Publishing, 1992) 81.

[5] Steichen, *Ungodly Rage*, (San Francisco: Ignatius Press, 1991) 160.

[6] Francis A. Schaeffer, *The Great Evangelical Disaster*, (Westchester, Illinois: Crossway Books, 1984) 136.

[7] Steichen, 193.

[8] ibid., 245.

[9] ibid., 284.

[10] ibid., 24.

[11] Goldberg, 20-21.

[12] *The Feminist Papers*, ed. Alice S. Rossi, (Boston: Northeastern University Press, 1973) 502.

[13] Cott, 107.

[14] Gilder, *Men and Marriage*, (Gretna: Pelican Publishing Co., 1986) 149-150.

[15] Steichen, 303.

[16] Cott, 273.

[17] Sommers, *Who Stole Feminism?*, (New York: Simon and Schuster, 1994) 275.

[18] Clark, 522.

[19] Alan Morrison, *The Serpent and the Cross*, (Birmingham, England: K&M Books, 1994) 329.

[20] Olasky, 67.

[21] ibid., 246.

[22] ibid., 246.

[23] Mitchell, *Weak Link*, (Washington: Regnery Gateway, 1989) 199.

[24] John Eidsmoe, *God and Caesar*, (Westchester, Illinois: Crossway Books, 1984) 110.

[25] Elliot, *Let Me Be a Woman*, (Wheaton: Tyndale House Publishers, 1976) 21.

[26] Elisabeth Elliot, *The Mark of a Man*, (Grand Rapids: Revell, 1981) 29.

[27] Weldon M. Hardenbrook, *Missing From Action*, (Nashville: Thomas Nelson, 1987) 147.

[28] Clark, 252.

[29] ibid., 162.

[30] Carroll Quigley, *The World Since 1939: A History*, (New York: Collier Books, 1968) 600.

[31] Friedan, *The Feminine Mystique*, (New York: Dell Publishing, 1983) 387.

[32] Kassian, *The Feminist Gospel*, (Wheaton: Crossway Books, 1992) 27.

[33] *The Feminist Papers*, 414.

[34] ibid., 460.

[35] Ratibor-Ray M. Jurjevich, *The Contemporary Faces of Satan*, (Denver: Ichthys Books, 1985) 274.

[36] Steichen, 74.

[37] Clark, 500, 501.

[38] Degler, *At Odds*, (New York: Oxford University Press, 1980) 343.

[39] ibid., 343.

[40] ibid., 352-353.

[41] Mark Twain, *The Diaries of Adam and Eve*, (New York: American Heritage Press, 1971) 9.

[42] Degler, 189.

[43] Steichen, 183.

[44] Sommers, 34, 35.

[45] Degler, 357-358.

[46] Green, 183.

[47] Kassian, 66.

[48] ibid., 61.

[49] ibid., 61.

[50] ibid., 61.

CHAPTER III
THE WEAKNESSES OF MEN

M en frequently want to dismiss feminism as a "woman thing"; as something to do with their menstrual cycle; as "their" problem not "ours." But, as in the Garden, eventually God is going to come to men and ask, "What happened?" Even if we have gotten the forbidden fruit of feminism from the hand of our mother, daughter, sister, wife or school teacher, still men are going to be asked to give an explanation for this overturning of God's created order. God is going to ask, "Where were you when My world, My home, and My church were being stood on their head (i.e., Christ)?" And the answer is going to be, "We were right there helping to push it over, Lord." This will have to be our answer because feminism appeals to the weaknesses of men and the weaknesses of men lead them to promote it.

By nature fallen man wants women to lead, to be ultimately responsible, to take charge. Historian Will Durant shows us this when he contrasts gender roles in ancient Babylon with those among God's people:

> In general the position of woman in Babylon was lower than in classic Greece or medieval Europe, and yet not worse than in classic Greece or medieval Europe. To carry out her many functions—begetting and rearing children, fetching water from the river or the public well, grinding corn, cooking, spinning, weaving, cleaning—she had to be free to be about in public very much like the man. She could own property, enjoy its income, sell and buy, inherit and bequeath. Some women kept shops, and carried on commerce;

some even became scribes, indicating that girls as well as boys might receive an education. *But the Semitic practice of giving almost limitless power to the oldest male of the family won out against matriarchal tendencies that may have existed in prehistoric Mesopotamia* (emphasis added).[1]

Of course, these practices did not just happen to "win out"—God mercifully preserved His created order in His people by means of His Spirit. But modern men, giving in to the spirit of the age rather than following the Holy Spirit, have given up God's created order in favor of Satan's order. They have abdicated headship, patriarchy, and responsibility for women in the name of liberty, equality, and justice. Men, having given up their proper position, make it all but impossible for women to occupy their God-given position. Furthermore, because the persistent desire of woman's fallen flesh is for the position of the man, she needs little encouragement to step into the void left by him.

Roman Catholic journalist Donna Steichen asserts that in order for women to have their God-given rights it is essential that patriarchy be restored.[2] This was also the conclusion of the great grandmother of feminism, Mary Wollstonecraft. She wrote as follows in her eighteenth century essay, "A Vindication of the Rights of Woman": "The conclusion I wish to draw is obvious; make women rational creatures, and free citizens, and they will quickly become good wives and mothers; that is—*if men do not neglect the duties of husbands and fathers*" (emphasis added).[3]

Sociologist Steven Goldberg comes to a similar conclusion. Women need men to be men in order for them to be women and vice versa. He says, "[E]very physiologically-rooted psychological tendency, every 'motivation' of the type we discuss [i.e. male dominance, female as nurturer], *requires an environmental cue and an environment in which the cued behavior can be manifested."*[4]

Modern men are not providing the cues or the environment for women to be women, and they do not do so because it is very appealing to their particular weaknesses as fallen men not to. And when men will not "wear the pants" in the family and/or they make it distasteful for women to "wear the dress" in the family, feminism is encouraged and flourishes.

The God-given role of man is headship. Therefore, his weaknesses will all relate to failures in this area. He fails at being the head when he does not care for women as their Creator would have them cared for and when he leads them in directions that God never intended them to go.

One of the most prevalent, persistent weaknesses of men is that they do not care properly for women. Martin Luther, the sixteenth century reformer, called women "that pitiable sex" not because of what *they* are but because of what *men* are; because of how men misused women.[5] In his lectures on Genesis he said that men using fallen human reason can "see nothing in the female sex but weakness and annoyance."[6] The perfect Adam cried out in joy upon seeing Eve, "At last! This one is bone of my bone, and flesh of my flesh!" We much-less-than-perfect men say, "Why do I have to take care of her?"

If only this was all—if only it was just that sinful men did not take care of women properly. If only men left them completely alone to fend for themselves, women would fair better than they do now. But this is not what happens. Men take care of women all right, but it is to *their* advantage. Fallen men demand their God-given authority *over* women, while abdicating or outright denying their God-given responsibility *for* women. Every married woman the author has talked to along these lines has been able to relate to this... including his wife. A husband will retain all the authority, claiming the right to dictate to her what to buy, decide, or do—even in minutia. But when things do not work out, whose fault is it? "Why, it is this woman You gave me Lord," men respond, showing they are true descendants of Adam. When men retain author-ity but deny responsibility, women are put in a truly 'no-win' situation. If they do not submit to their husband, they sin. If they do submit to a bad decision, they are held at fault by their husband. Such obvious, gross unfairness on the part of men pushes women toward feminist thinking, or even facilitates their conversion to feminism.

The classic sexual double standard is another case of men claiming authority without accepting corresponding responsibility. Men want the freedom, the absolute authority, to do what they want sexually before marriage; many men expect understanding of their "uncontrollable" sexual drive even during marriage. The famous and much-revered English writer Samuel Johnson wrote in 1768 England that a wife is more guilty than a husband if she is unfaithful because of the confusion of progeny. He goes on to say that a wife ought not to greatly resent an unfaithful husband who uses the maid; in fact, it is her fault if her husband resorts to a maid or harlot. To prove the sincerity of his remarks, Johnson says that he would not take in a daughter who left her husband because of sexual escapades.[7] With such a view already *publicly* advocated by respectable men in 1768, is it any wonder that feminist Charlotte Gilman could write as follows in 1898? "The absolutely stationary female and the wide ranging male are distinctly human institutions..."[8]

No, they were not "human institutions"—they were dysfunctional, sinful human institutions set up long ago by fallen men. Already in Genesis 38, the patriarch Judah saw nothing wrong with requiring celibacy of his widowed daughter-in-law, Tamar, while allowing himself a tryst with a prostitute. When his double standard was exposed, Judah repented. He took responsibility for Tamar and ceased from exercising his authority over her for his benefit.

The Church has never accepted a double standard in favor of men over against women. She has never advocated men having authority without the corresponding responsibility. Fourth century church father Gregory of Nazianzus knew of customs and laws that, "restrained the woman, but indulged the man," that penalized the adulterous woman but did not hold the adulterous man accountable. He says forcefully in response to these: "I do not accept this legislation; I do not approve this custom."[9]

The fathers of the Church did not back away from the God-given hierarchy, the God-given gender roles with all their ramifications. Listen to what St. Ambrose wrote in the fourth century: "Woman must respect her husband, not be a slave to him; she consents to be ruled, not to be forced. The one whom a yoke would fit is not fit for the yoke of marriage. As to man, he should guide his wife like a pilot, honor her as a partner in life, share with her as co-heir of grace." And in another work, "How great is the power of marriage, that the stronger is also at the service of the other."[10]

When the church fathers speak of "authority over" they almost always do so in the context of "responsibility for"; they realize God gave men authority so that their responsibility for women could be carried out and that men were responsible for an equal not an inferior. But when feminists, and others, read these church fathers, and they find the words "inferior" and "superior" in the context of the relationship between the sexes, they conclude wrongly that the Church has been sexist.

Popular writer Elisabeth Elliot explains that these words and concepts in Scripture (and therefore in the fathers as well) originally made reference to *position*—not to *intrinsic worth*.[11] It is the same with the words "master" and "slave" in the Scriptures. These terms could not have been regarded by St. Paul, and certainly not by God, as descriptions of a person's intrinsic worth. If they were, how could Paul have sent, with divine authority, masters and slaves back into such a system? Words like "master" and "slave," "inferior" and "superior" were terms of relationship. These words, these concepts, did not alter the intrinsic equality that both had in God's sight and should have had in the sight of one another.[12] That this is St. Paul's view can be seen in reading those passages where he exalts the high relationship that is to obtain between master and slave and husband and wife. That this is exactly the view we find in the church fathers can be seen in a homily by Chrysostom: "For what if the wife be under subjection to us? It is as a wife, as free, as equal in honor."[13]

But because of the sinful weaknesses of men, we find men asserting, or more often simply assuming, their right to have a woman submit to them without their having any responsibility to her as one free and equal in honor to them. This is why we find Abigail Adams writing to her husband John in 1776, "Men of sense in all ages abhor those customs which treat us only as vassals of your sex. Regard us then as Beings placed by Providence under your protection and in imitation of the Supreme Being make use of that power only for our happiness."[14] Evidently colonial men did just that (or were at least close to this ideal) because the four primary sources of depression women in a 1980s survey listed did not exist among colonial women. Mary Ryan, a professor of history, says that low self-esteem, fatigue and time pressures, loneliness, and absence of romance in marriage were unknown among colonial women.[15]

"Ah ha," today's conservative man will declare, "If women had just not become feminists then they would still have it as good today as colonial women did then!" But it was the weaknesses of men—not the feminism of women—that got the ball rolling. Women were not the ones who started abandoning their homes—*men* did that. (Only Christian men did not.) Women were not the ones who started indulging in casual sex—*men* always did. (Only Christian men did not.) Women learned from the weaknesses of men how to upset God's creation. A 1950 novel has a female character expressing it well, "I know this is hard to explain to a man.

But I've wanted a man's power always to use as I liked with my woman's brain..."[16]

When men do not use their power, authority, position, role, and strength to take responsibility for women, women suffer. And if necessity is the mother of invention, a mother in necessity will do incredible things for those *she* feels responsible for—her children. So the nineteenth century woman increasingly turned to divorce. "It was not that women rejected the home, for the vast majority of them certainly did not, not even those who petitioned for divorce. What an increasing proportion of women did insist upon, so the records of divorce tell us, was a recognition of their proper role in the home without undue subordination."[17]

Women did not reject the home; men in their sinful weakness did. They insisted on subordination without taking responsibility for women. As an indication of how bad things were in the nineteenth century, please note the first annual report of the U.S. Department of Agriculture dated 1863. It condemned farmers for not treating their wives as people—let alone as women.[18] This is how Captain Bly treated the sailors of the *Bounty*, and no one wonders why they mutinied.

The cry from the equity feminists (as opposed to the radical feminists who seek to overthrow all patriarchal institutions) is that if women do not look out for themselves men will not do it for them. And truthfully, it is *not* a feminist position to call for men to take proper care for the real needs of women and children—it is a civilized one.[19] Where men are being properly responsible for women, feminists do not gain much of a hearing. Betty Friedan admits as much in remarking about Susan B. Anthony's nineteenth century petition for married women's right to own property. "[H]alf the time even the women slammed doors in their faces with the smug remark that they had husbands, they needed no laws to protect them."[20]

In 1915 the suffragists insisted on the vote, "because

men, even good men, cannot be trusted to take care of women's interests."[21] Given the track record of men, who can gainsay this opinion? Does it not seem that the solution *is* to give women the authority, the right, the power to take care of themselves? Of course, it does. This is reasonable; this is practical; and, to some degree, it works. This is feminism, and the weakness of men—to deny responsibility for women while demanding authority over them—makes it very hard for women to resist it.

Men have promoted feminism by failing to take care of women in the way in which God intended. Nowhere is this more evident than in the area of sexuality. The weakness of men in this particular area shows up in three distinct ways: 1) by men accepting and/or promoting anything that leads to their having more unhindered access to an unaccountable enjoyment of sex; 2) by men exalting an individual woman's sexuality while demeaning women as a group; and 3) by men loving a woman's sexuality while ignoring where that flows from (personality) and undervaluing where it flows to (wifedom and motherhood).

Everyone admits that a sexual revolution was brought about by the feminist movement. But truthfully, men had revolted against God's understanding of sexuality *long* before feminism. Without condoning it and while calling it sinful, we must admit that historically men have been, for the most part, more sexually "available." Feminists were not the first to revolt against God's sexual order; men were. Feminism merely claimed this same sexual availability for women, and men loved it.

It is to the shame of men that we are so weak sexually. The great sexual sinners of the Bible are all men; this despite the fact that men have done their best to make women like Eve and Mary Magdalene sexual sinners even though Scripture does not say one word in this direction. The great sexual sinners of the Bible are all men; Judah, David, Amnon and Lot were all overcome by sexual lust and committed the most reprehensible sins. Judah slept with a woman he believed to be a cult prostitute. David seduced one man's only wife while he himself had an entire harem from which to choose. Amnon raped his half-sister knowing that his father would not have refused to give her to him as wife. And Lot considered the rape of his daughters as being preferable to the homosexual rape of visitors, and then, while under the influence of alcohol and lust, he engaged in incest on two consecutive nights.

It is not an accident that when our Lord applied the Sixth Commandment, He said, "Whosoever looks at a woman to lust after her has committed adultery with her already in his heart." The omniscient Lord did not think that women do not lust, but had He particularly pointed the commandment at women, it would not have rung true in the hearts of men or women.

Conventional and Biblical wisdom have recognized men's glaring sexual weakness. This is the source of sayings such as, "A bad woman will sooner turn a good man's heart than a bad man will a good woman's." This is why the eighteenth century British statesmen Chesterfield advised his son, "[E]ven powerful statesmen are influenced by weak women, especially if these are not their wives."[22] And this is why the Bible's Book of Proverbs warns many times of loose, adulterous, promiscuous women but never once of promiscuous men. It is not that there are so many promiscuous women, but that *men*, being so weak in this area, must be constantly on guard against falling for licentious women. And it is not that women are so strong that they do not need to be warned about promiscuous men, but that promiscuous men are the norm; women do not need to be warned about what is so commonplace.

Society has traditionally, but wrongly, had to depend on the virtue of women to counterbalance the sexual weakness of men. George Gilder bluntly says,

The crucial process of civilization is the subordination

of male sexual impulses and biology to the long-term horizon of female sexuality. The overall sexual behavior of women in the world differs relatively little from the sexual life of women in primitive societies. It is male behavior that must be changed to create a civilized order.[23]

This is not, however, a startling modern discovery. In colonial times, John Adams observed a similar thing, saying: "The Jews, the Greeks, the Romans, the Swiss, the Dutch, all lost their public Spirit, their Republican Principles and habits, and their Republican Forms of Government when they lost the Modesty and Domestic Virtues of their Women..."[24]

Now Americans have "lost the modest and domestic virtues of their women," but the loss did not occur when most of us think it did. Feminist Suzanne LaFollette said it was gone already in 1926, and she linked the loss to the fact that men never had it—but is that not in essence what John Adams admitted by his remarks? This is what LaFollette had to say:

Of late there has been much public discussion of the wantonness of our modern youth; which, being interpreted, means the disposition of our girls to take the same liberty of indulgence in pre-nuptial sexual affairs that has been countenanced in boys. The tendency is an entirely natural result of woman's increased freedom.[25]

This is the fulfillment of sinful men's dreams: to have women as sexually weak-willed as they are; to have women who are willing to be as irresponsible about sex as they are; to have women committed to self-gratification as much as they are. Why is feminism so hard to resist? Because it promotes and produces the kind of women which sinful, sexually weak men like to have around, and so it appeals to a weakness of men that has ruined families, churches, and even nations for eons. Earlier, the author quoted a woman in a novel who always wanted a man's power to use with a woman's brain. Well, sinful men would love to be surrounded by female bodies being used by a man's brain. This is what feminism gives them, so men are constantly pulled toward tolerating, promoting, or advocating feminism.

The sexual weakness of a man leads individual women—perhaps his very wife and daughter(s)—towards feminism. His weakness is not merely that he accepts and promotes whatever leads to having more access to, and enjoyment of. irresponsible sex, but consistently he exalts an individual woman's beauty and sexuality while simultaneously demeaning women as a group. For example, men will make jokes about the stupidity and vanity of the beauty pageant mentality while drooling over the bathing suit competition.

This sort of reaction by men can trap a woman into thinking of herself as a sex object. After all, this seems to be (and, unfortunately, all too frequently is) the only way men, even her own husband, value her. Once a woman buys into this, she buys, quite literally, into a great many other things: clothes, cosmetics, jewelry, hair coloring/styling, and even surgery. Believing she is valued primarily for her outward appearance, her "sex appeal," she does everything she can to embellish, prolong, or even fake it.

But what happens when a woman does not have much to embellish? What happens when a woman cannot prolong it any longer? What happens when a woman recognizes the hollowness of faking it? Where does she have to go for comfort, for consolation, for understanding? Is it any wonder that women are driven toward feminism where outward appearance is not the main issue and most of the time not even an issue at all?

Of course, women ought to be able to turn toward the Church. Christians serve a God who does not regard the face or the body of a man or a woman when dealing with a person. Christians have been told by their God that they are not to judge by outward appearances. Within the Church, among Christians, appearance should not be an issue at all, let alone a primary one in regard to how men and women relate to one another. In fact, in regards to women, the Lord of the Church has told us in Proverbs 30 and I Peter 3 *not* to let their outward adorning be the issue. God even calls beauty a vain (that is, a futile, empty) thing, in Proverbs 30! The only place a woman's beauty is mentioned as being an issue is in Song of Solomon, and there, as it should be, beauty is in the eyes of the beholder.

Perhaps the founder of modern feminism, Betty Friedan, was not so far from the mark when she said,

> It is my thesis that the core of the problem for women today is not sexual but a problem of identity—a stunting or evasion of growth that is perpetuated by the feminine mystique. It is my thesis that as the Victorian culture did not permit women to accept or gratify their basic sexual needs, our culture does not permit women to accept or gratify their basic need to grow and fulfill their potentialities as human beings, a need which is not solely defined by their sexual role.[26]

The problem is all wrapped up with sexuality and personhood. Women are driven towards places where they can exist and will be recognized as more than sexual beings. Feminism purports to be one such place; the Church should be another.

What drives a woman toward feminism faster than solely valuing her for sexual reasons is criticizing her gender. Women quickly tire of men who value them as individuals, more often than not for sexual reasons, but are constantly at war with the opposite sex. They are particularly upset when their gender is attacked for behavior inspired by men's values.

For example, since the nineteenth century, a magazine will contain articles criticizing women for shallowness, vanity, and immodest dress, but, at the same time it will be chocked full of advertisements showing individual woman surrounded by silly products with perfectly painted faces, low neck lines, and big breasts. Women, rightly so, are very sensitive to this schizophrenia of which men are so capable. How can their husband really prize them as individuals and detest the group they belong to by nature? How can their husband drool over sexuality (even their own) yet detest women for pursuing sex appeal?

The Church has certainly been guilty of looking down on women as a group. Thomas Aquinas said that a woman was an "imperfect man" and an "incidental being."[27] Martin Luther, calls it "a foolish law of the Pope" when he chides the Roman Catholic church of the sixteenth century for teaching that a woman could not wash an altar linen that the body of Christ had lain on unless it was first washed by a pure priest.[28]

The Church is guilty in modern times, too. As late as 1983, the question of women communing during their menstrual period had not been settled in many Orthodox parishes. This despite the fact that a second century work, *The Teaching of the Twelve Apostles*, specifically addresses this issue, saying it is wrong to prevent menstruating women from communing.[29] The author has heard Lutherans say that they did not think that women, because of their gender, should handle the sacramental elements after the service. One cannot help but think of portraits showing the removal of the body of Christ from the cross and how the women then touched and handled His most sacred body.

Organized religion has been, and still is in some ways, guilty of denigrating women as a group. But this is much more true of the world than it ever was of Christianity. For example, historians Will and Ariel Durant tell us that in the eighteenth century "enlightened" English women in all classes were looked down upon as naturally and irrevocably inferior to men.[30] In limiting the rights of women, Romans cited the imbecility and instability of the sex.[31] Aristotle said,

"The female is female by virtue of a certain *lack* of qualities." And, "We should regard the female nature as afflicted with a natural defectiveness"(emphasis original).[32]

The most stunning remarks, however, come from the nineteenth century when mankind supposedly made so much progress scientifically. According to the nineteenth century view of things, biological changes in adolescent males produce a physically stronger individual, but such changes in adolescent females were regarded as having the opposite effect.[33] Harvard physician Horatio Storer said in 1875, "[T]here is this inherent quality in their sex, month to month in each woman, that unfits her from taking those responsibilities which are to control questions of life and death."[34] Feminist Antoinette Brown Blackwell, also writing in 1875, laid the blame for such idiotic thinking where it should be placed: not on the doctrines of the Church, but on the doctrine of evolution. She said that it was the expounders of evolution, Spencer and Darwin, who were the ones who argued that women are inferior to men.[35]

A woman is constantly confronted with profoundly contradictory attitudes in men. A man will cherish her individually yet demean women as a group, and he will use any of her individual flaws as proof the group is flawed, too. The first woman on the civil service commission said in the 1920s: "[A]ny woman's failure is held against all women, but a man's failure is his individual weakness." Likewise, outstanding women are viewed as an exception to their sex.[36] But outstanding men are regarded as the perfection of their sex.

The gender polarity that God has created in human beings causes men to value women *because* they are different. This is part of the sexual tension. Obviously, men value the difference in this area, but they seldom do anywhere else. For example, rather than saying women's emotions function differently than men's emotions, men say women are more emotional.[37] Rather than saying women make decisions differently than men do, men say women are indecisive. Writing in the 1880s, feminist Mary Austin described men's thinking in this regard. "There was a human norm...and it was the average man. Whatever in woman differed from this norm was a female weaknesses, of intelligence, of character, of physique" (emphasis original).[38]

The weakness of men to love individual women, especially for their sexuality, but to look down on women as a group has made feminism impossible for many women to resist. This weakness of men has also caused much pain for many women. Women need to know they are loved as a group, as a gender. Martin Luther said as much in his lectures on Genesis when he quoted two sayings of his day: "One should praise women, whether it be true or false; they have need of it." "Many a man speaks ill of women who does not know what his mother did."[39]

Women have endured much suffering through the ages even in relatively modern times. A well known Texas proverb testifies to this: Texas was, "a heaven for men and dogs, but a hell for women and oxen." This proverb originated in the mind of an old lady.[40] Often a woman's only source of solace was Christianity. Consider the case of feminist poet Alice Cary, who died a miserable death in 1871. Her biographer tells us that only when hearing those portions of the Gospel which tell of Christ's love for women was she happy in her suffering.[41]

Those portions are quite large, are they not? "To be born of a virgin He doth not despise," we sing in popular carol. Christ deigned to show Himself to the aged, widowed Anna. He sought out the woman at the well. He raised the only son of the widow of Nain. He personally took the time to stop by Mary and Martha's house to teach them. He put the news of the resurrection in the mouths of women. And He rebuked His disciples on Easter evening, not because they deserted Him, but, "because they believed not them [the women] which had seen Him after He was risen" (Mark 16:14).

The weakness of men—exalting a woman's sexuality while demeaning women as a group—pushes women toward feminism. The weakness of men to make a woman's sexuality an end in itself also does this. Men do this in two ways: by ignoring where a woman's sexuality flows from (personality) and by undervaluing where a woman's sexuality flows to (wifedom/motherhood).

Women struggle to be regarded by men as persons, not objects to be used (whether to satisfy sexual desires or complete household tasks). Once more, this problem is traceable to the nineteenth century. Betty Friedan laments the concept of that era known as *femme couverte*, which means "covered woman." She say, according to nineteenth century feminists, it suspended, "'the very being or legal existence of a woman' upon marriage."[42]

Our Lord does call upon both man and woman to sacrifice self to each other, but neither ceases to be a person in the relationship. If either did, then two could not be one in marriage. Human beings can only be one with another person; animals, created beings without personhood, will not do. God knew this from the very beginning. It was no surprise to Him when no helper was found suitable to the man out of all the animals in the Garden. Michelangelo's Sistine Chapel painting reflects this beautifully: when God is reaching out with the index finger of His right hand to impart the spark of life to Adam, you can see tucked under His left arm the already created Eve. Woman was by no means an afterthought, a second-class creation. As Genesis puts it so beautifully, "So God created man in His own image, in the image of God created He him; male and female created He them" (Genesis 1:27).

But even perfect man had to be taught this. God knew from the beginning that it was not good for man to be alone, but God had to bring this realization out in Adam. He did this by parading all the animals before Adam to show *him* none were suitable for him. He could not be one with any of them because none of the animals were personal beings. So when husbands explicitly or implicitly deny the personhood of their wife, they are standing in the way of the oneness God has given them in creation and in the marriage bond.

To be treated as a non-person is very painful. Two nineteenth century novels show the problem and the pain. Sir Walter Scott says in *Ivanhoe*, "Women are but toys which amuse our lighter hours..." Toys are objects without personality except, of course, when a child invests a toy with the personality he wishes it to have. This is what men in their sinful weakness do to women, particularly their spouses. They give a woman the personality they wish her to have rather than finding out (and rejoicing in) the one they do have. Women in despair frequently say to their spouse, "You don't even know me."

The second nineteenth century novelist to describe the problem and the pain of being an invisible person is Nathaniel Hawthorne. In *The Scarlet Letter*, he describes women who have the "dreary burden" of, "a heart unyielded, because unvalued and unsought." Too many men seek their bodies, not their hearts, and the weakness of sinful men is they can be satisfied with just the body.

Men in the nineteenth century already noticed the despondency of women, but concluded it had nothing to do with their hearts. The Philadelphia College of Medicine said,

> Women's reproductive organs are pre-eminent. They exercise a controlling influence upon her entire system, and entail upon her many painful and dangerous diseases. They are the source of her peculiarities, the center of her sympathies, and the seat of her diseases. Everything that is peculiar to her springs from her sexual organization.[43]

To be sure, there is something connected to the sinful weakness of women as women that leads them towards depression and despondency so much more frequently than most men. To be sure their mood swings have something to do with hormones and the reproductive cycle. But the view expressed by the Philadelphia College of Medicine completely dismisses women as people, as personalities, as individuals. In effect, this nineteenth century medical "diagnosis" reduces women to animals. Animals are controlled by instincts. Animal behavior, not human behavior, is determined by reproductive organs. Animal "moods" are controlled by "ruts" and "heats" and estrus cycles.

If we understand a woman's behavior in this way, we are calling her an animal, and we will dismiss or discount her thoughts, opinions, ideas, and abilities and we will do so throughout her whole life. She is either "having her period," "has one in the oven," or is going through "her change of life." Interestingly enough, it is witchcraft, which much of radical feminism follows and eagerly embraces, that focuses on the life cycle of woman, dividing it into the maiden, mother, and crone. By doing so, they are unknowingly returning to the nineteenth century view that a woman's life *is* her reproductive cycle. If men do dismiss what a woman thinks, feels, or is, then they cannot relate to and will not address the situation that Betty Friedan wrote about in 1963: the empty, aching wondering if there is something more.

When men (husbands in particular) discount a woman's "bad days" as "female problems," women are driven to others who will treat them as persons—counselors, lovers, and feminists. But many women come to believe that the counselor is treating them as a person for money, and most women come to find out that their lover is doing so for sex. This leaves the feminists as the only choice.

A historian has said that the issue with the suffragists of the early twentieth century was whether women should be treated as individuals or as subordinates who served the family.[44] While women are to subordinate themselves to their husband, they are not a subordinate of his and certainly in no sense of the family! Subordinates are not "persons"; they are not usually selected for their personality traits, but for what they do. Subordinates perform functions. A functional view of womanhood leaves them without personhood.

It is true; the nineteenth century woman did struggle to be a person. But this was not the case for the women of the seventeenth and eighteenth centuries. For example, the literature from these eras which deals with sex considered pleasure a normal and necessary part of intercourse for women. There was a general expectation that it was fitting and proper for women to *personally* enjoy sex. However, nineteenth century books did not have this expectation; in them, sex was a base human drive that women should not find pleasure in.[45] D.H. Lawrence's novel *Lady Chatterley's Lover*, written in 1928, is a rebellion against this view. The protagonist is a man who only values women who personally enjoy sex. Unfortunately the work is also a rebellion against marital love.

There is a link between personhood and sexuality. If women are not regarded as people by men, then men should not expect them to enjoy their sexuality. In other words, in missing their personhood, their true sexuality is also missed. Sexuality is not merely (or even mostly) bound up in a woman's physical anatomy or outward beauty as our pornographic culture would lead women and men to believe; sexuality is bound up in a woman's personality. If sex were only a matter of anatomy and not also personality then inflatable plastic women would do. The fact that hundreds of thousands of such "plastic" women have been sold only proves the point: Women have been depersonalized in the eyes of many men.

But who makes "blow-up" men for sex toys for women? No one, because for women sex flows from personality. One might say that they cannot imagine sex without it. Men can and do. However, because of the weakness of men, millions of women have depersonalized sex because they have sex with a man who regards them as little more than a plastic woman.

If men want to understand how a woman feels when a man does not regard her personhood but only her anatomy, he only need ponder the fact that inflatable men are sold *for security*. To feel more secure, a woman can use a personality-free plastic man to ride in her car or sit in her home. But when it comes to sharing a life or a bed, women crave something more than a plastic man. This is not a weakness of women; it is a fact. It is a weakness of men that they ignore this fact or do not take the time to appreciate it.

Men value sexuality very highly in women even though they ignore the personality it flows from. This drives women to feminist thinking, and so does the fact that men demean where the sexuality of their women flows to: motherhood.

Chrysostom, in his homily number 20 from the Book of Ephesians, says that although God could have given the gift of childbearing to Adam He gave it to Eve to keep Adam from pride in his own priority.[46] Adam valued Eve very much as the bearer of children. Genesis 3:20 tells us, "And Adam called his wife's name Eve; because she was the mother of all the living."

Modern man does not value women as the bearers of children. If you look at seventeenth and eighteenth century paintings of women, you will notice that many of them—even a majority of them—portray women with characteristics typical of women who have borne children: prominent hips where many a child has rested, distended, round bellies pouched out by children growing in the womb, and nipples that have obviously nursed them. Maternal beauty is exalted in these paintings. The ideal woman is one whose body shows the telltale traits of childbearing.

Contrast this with the ideal woman of the present century: skinny almost to the point of being emaciated, no stretch marks, hips that jeans barely rest on (let alone children!), breasts that are either adolescently small or extremely big, and nipples that have never nursed. The "ideal" woman is one that is out of reach for 99 percent of mothers.

Can this dramatic change in the ideal woman be traced to the nineteenth century, the century that exalted motherhood covering it with sentimentality and devoting a special day each year to it? I believe it can. The nineteenth century made a false dichotomy between motherhood and sexuality with the point being implicitly made that to be maternal was not to be sexual and *vice versa*. But motherhood is the God-given fruition of sexuality. A mother who enjoys her sexuality is really being true to her Creator, but not in the nineteenth century. Motherhood stood aloof, above, too 'holy' for sexuality, and, therefore, motherhood denied being the goal of sexuality. So sexuality became something to be endured rather than enjoyed. But the same thing happens when you deny the goal of sexuality (motherhood) as when you deny the source (personality): true female sexuality is lost. It was lost or at least sublimated in the nineteenth century, but it was left to the radical feminism of the twentieth century to provide a place for women who have lost their true female sexuality. It is called Lesbianism.

The nineteenth century false dichotomy between sexuality and motherhood placed women in a no-win situation: they were told they must be healthy and robust to be good mothers to their children, but they had to be pale and delicate to be sexually attractive to men.[47] The distinctive feminine dress of the Victorian era was designed with the intent of achieving both goals simultaneously. It was fashioned to accent a woman's maternal ability while at the same time sexually stimulate men: "Corsets distorted women's bodies to stress their procreative functions. Tight lacing pushed the breasts up and enlarged them visually by shrinking the size of the waist." Bustles hoops gave the illusion of an enlarged pelvis which would be fertile and provide for easy delivery.[48] The large hoops gave men an enticing eyeful when the ladies walked up the stairs while the pushed up breasts gave them a beguiling view from the stairs at the women below. All of this was by design.

The real irony of all this is that although the Victorian dress succeeded in making women sexually alluring, it actually hurt women's health and even damaged their childbearing ability.[49] One cannot help but think of women who pursue their sexuality today with such vengeance that they, too, harm their health, if not their childbearing ability. (Think of tanning parlors, unhealthy dieting, tight jeans that cut off circulation, high heels that hurt backs, etc.)

Already in the eighteenth century feminists began rebelling against the false dichotomy between sexuality and motherhood that the weakness of men pushed them to pursue. Here is what the *grande dame* of feminism, Mary Wollstonecraft, had to say on this subject:

> Nature has given woman a weaker frame than man; but to ensure her husband's affections, must a wife, who by the exercise of her mind and body whilst she was discharging the duties of a daughter, wife, and mother, has allowed her constitution to retain its natural strength, and her nerves a healthy tone, is she, I say to condescend to use art and feign a sickly delicacy in order to secure her husband's affections?[50]

Eighteenth century feminism, as documented earlier, began a crusade for the better treatment of women in the areas of marriage and mothering. Women wanted proper respect and care so they might be better wives and mothers, not so they might be independent of husband and children. Abigail Adams demanded in 1776 that "particular care and attention" be paid to women for this reason and warned that if not, "we are determined to foment a Rebellion."[51]

Particular attention was not paid, and women did rebel. They rebelled precisely according to the way men in their weakness, valued them. The History of Woman Suffrage (written in 1880) is proof. According to this history, "Womanhood is the great fact in her life; wifehood and motherhood are but incidental relations."[52] Men valued women for their "woman-hood" (i.e., sexuality), and rather than viewing wifehood and motherhood as the goals of their sexuality, men viewed them as incidentals. Women learned what men had taught them, and emphasized what men always did.

This takes us all the way back to the fact that men will accept and promote anything that gives them more access to sex without responsibility. Once women gave up the goal of marriage and motherhood in reaction to how men treated (or, more accurately, mistreated) these things, sex was no longer rooted in these things, either. Sex need not be saved for these things; the goal of sexuality for women could become just what it had always been for sinful, weak, fallen men: self and self-gratification.

Now women were free to use sex like sinful men always had, and this was the true sexual revolution. The sexual revolution was not that people started to jump in and out of bed with each other at the drop of a hat, but that women felt freed to use sex in ways that fallen men always had. Men brought this revolution about by sinfully neglecting the goal of women's sexuality (motherhood). But this revolution did not hurt men at all personally. In fact, it fed right into their appetite for uncommitted, unaccountable, easy sex. No wonder feminism is so hard to resist—it helps to feed an insatiable appetite of fallen men.

Feminism is so hard to resist because of the weakness of men in *caring* for women properly and because of their weakness in *leading* women properly. It all comes down to headship. God created and ordained man the head. Therefore, his sinful weaknesses will relate to failures in that area in some fashion. Having looked at how fallen men have failed to care for women properly, we turn our attention to their failure to lead them properly. It is not just that men have failed to lead properly, but they have actually led women in the wrong direction.

It seems to have started with men casting off authority and hierarchy—the very things women are now engaged in throwing off. First, men became uncomfortable with the thought of God being over them, then of other men being over them, and then with men being over women. With the children's rights movement, we have come to the point where men are uncomfortable being over even children. This all came about because, "we have been drowned in a flood of liberation ideology." Liberation ideology has taught us that headship has no connotation of authority and hierarchy really means tyranny.[53]

Did men or women buy into the ideology of liberation first? Men did. Then certain women parroted back that ideology, and men—who had already co-opted two-thirds of God's hierarchy (church and state) by rebellion—could not very well maintain the third part (home) for long. Feminists toppled the hierarchy completely because that was the direction in which men had already gotten the cart to lean.

But not merely an order fell. When the order gave way, then men became less masculine and women less feminine. A reversal of roles was set in motion. An earlier chapter referred to the Sheppard-Towner bill of 1921, the first bill passed after women won the franchise. This bill was the first law directing that public funds were to be used for social welfare. Although at that time the congress was, for all practical purposes, still all-male, it was a feminized congress that passed the bill, nevertheless. However, one of the few vocal opponents of the bill was a woman, Alice Richardson, a one-term congresswoman from Oklahoma. She openly belittled the statistics provided by the children's bureau as "sob stuff," said the bill was nothing more than German paternalism, and that it would eventually drain the treasury.[54]

Alice Richardson should be regarded as something of a prophetess. The social welfare spending that began in 1921 really picked up steam in the 1930s and 1960s, and now it can be said that we have spent enough money on such programs to buy every Fortune 500 company and every piece of farmland in America.[55] The only reason we have not drained the treasury as Richardson predicted is because of the miracle of deficit spending whereby we can spend what we do not have. However, the main point in all of this is that it was a woman and not a man who took up the cause against a feminine use of government funds.

This reversal of roles can be seen in the area of dress, too. It is not just that women are dressing more like men, but men are dressing more like women. It is perfectly acceptable and even very fashionable for a man or a woman to dress more like the opposite sex. We see this as mere fashion or taste; the early church, however, saw it as cursed and pagan. The Council of Nicea in 325 A.D. said, "If any woman, under pretense of asceticism, shall change her apparel and instead of a woman's accustomed clothing, shall put on that of man, let her be anathema."[56]

Men have not only tolerated the masculinizing of women and the feminizing of men in dozens of ways, they have led all of society in that direction. The responsibility falls on men not only because God made them head and tolerates no abdications, but because the degree to which women take power is inverse to the degree to which men let it go. Where there is a Deborah judging Israel, you will find a Barak reluctant to assume the headship. As a convert to Catholicism liked to observe, "St. Joseph was least of the Holy Family, but its head."[57] Modern men quite frequently make themselves the most in their family but in the least its head.

In His wisdom, God made man the spiritual head; he is suppose to lead, to exercise the authority, to assume the responsibility in spiritual matters. Women are not to lead, exercise authority over men, or take responsibility; they are to be subordinate, to stand under, to submit to male headship. Some church fathers offered explanations for this. Chrysostom's explanation, without a doubt, would offend many women today—let alone feminists. He said that the cause of the women being in subjection was, "...the woman is in some sort a weaker being and easily carried away and light-minded."[58] This may sound sharp even to ears that wish to listen to only the voice of the Good Shepherd, until we remember that St. Paul finds two reasons for the women not to exercise authority over men: "Because Adam was first formed, then Eve. And Adam was not deceived, but the women being deceived [literally "being thoroughly deceived"] was in the transgression" (I Timothy 2: 13, 14).

Also it must be remembered that feminists themselves are adamant that men and women think differently. The differences they see strike one as being in the same vein as Chrysostom's phrase "easily carried away and light-minded." For example, feminist theologians often identify a masculine and a feminine side of God. The masculine side of God, according to them, is objective, rational, intellectual perception. The feminine side, according to them, is subjective, intuitive experience.[59] All throughout feminism, one finds woman exalted for being superior to man in the areas of feeling, emoting, and sensing. She is regarded as being superior spiritually in that she is gifted in extrasensory perception rather than sensory perception as the man is.[60] This definitely sounds similar to the trait that Chrysostom described as "light-minded."

It sounds the same way to equity feminist Christina Hoff Sommers. She notes that among gender feminists there is an "implacable hostility to all exact thinking as 'male'."[61] This is found even among the very best educated feminists. In academia, feminists who have as their goal to free the world of all oppression are known as transformationists. But these highly educated women view logic and rationality as "phallocentric"; they consider "conceptions of rationality and intelligence as white male creations."[62] Sommers castigates the feminist classroom saying, "While male students are off studying such 'vertical' subjects as engineering and biology, women in feminist classrooms are sitting around being 'safe' and 'honoring' feelings."[63]

Sommers rails against this saying that this only "plays into old sexist stereotypes that extol women's capacity for intuition, emotion, and empathy while denigrating their capacity to think objectively and systematically in the way men can."[64] But could it be that even the radical gender feminists are forced to confess the truth that men and women really do think differently? Could it be that women really are gifted for different things than men are? Could it be that the analytical, systematic, precise thinking which sound theology requires is not a gift given to women? Could it be that her gifts really do lie in the area of intuition, emotion, and empathy?

Having said this, let us hasten to add that we do not believe these very real differences between men and women are the reason spiritual headship was given to the male; even St. Paul does not say that. St. Paul states that women are not permitted to teach or have authority over men and that they are to be silent in the Church, but he does not say that this is because there are innate differences between men and women. He does say that Adam fell without being deceived while Eve was thoroughly deceived, but he does not say why there was this difference.

If we argue that God placed women where He did because of their different gifts, we are in the realm of human reason, and therefore, we are on very unstable ground. Men can easily be toppled by arguments from reason. For example, the feminist argument that women's particular gifts make them more suited for spiritual leadership than men has swayed many a man ruled by his fallen reason rather than by clear Scripture to give in and advocate spiritual leadership for women.

But God does not give a reason for male headship. He simply states the facts of how things should be. Spiritual headship and authority does not belong to women. It is not given to them but to men. This order is to prevail because—and only because—God in His wisdom wanted it this way. Birds fly, men do not; fish get their oxygen from water, men do not; men lead, women do not. To question why men lead is as useless as questioning why humans do not get their oxygen from water or why they do not fly.

This, however, does not stop prideful human reason. It hisses, "But do we not need a woman's point of view?" Deborah Belonick sees the fatal flaw in this enticing argument:

> Women in other fields may make great contributions to them by offering the 'woman's point of view'...but the same cannot be said of the field of theology. This is not because women are less correct as theologians, but because God is not determined by human thought and reasoning.[65]

Bobnick is absolutely right. God is not determined by human thought or reasoning. He does not fit within our parameters, whether these parameters are male or female. What is determinative for God is not a woman's or a man's viewpoint, but His own. However, if Belonick equates "theologian" with "spiritual leader," then she is wrong about women not being "less correct as theologians." Once more human reason will have to bow before God and admit that it is not given to women to be spiritual leaders, and therefore, she is always "less correct" if she tries to be one. This may not make sense to us, but we, as Reformation theologian Martin Luther said, endeavor to give the Holy Spirit the honor of knowing more than we do.

God gave spiritual headship to men, but the sinful weakness of men caused them to lead women toward spiritual leadership. Although we cannot know for sure, it seems that this is a replay of what went on in the Garden of Eden. Does not Genesis 3 give the impression that while Eve is dialoguing with the devil, Adam is close by saying nothing and thereby implicitly abdicating his spiritual headship? Then he does it explicitly by following Eve into sin even though he is no way deceived, as she was, as to the horrible consequences of his actions.

Once more we must journey back to the nineteenth century if we wish to find out how men surrendered their spiritual headship in modern times. To be sure, eighteenth century man was already leaning that way, as a poem by Alexander Pope written for Lady Mary Wortley Montagu shows:

> Then bravely, fair dame,/ Resume the old claim,/ Which to your whole sex does belong;/ And let men receive/ From a second bright Eve/ The knowledge of right and wrong./ But if the first Eve/ Hard doom did receive/ When only one apple had she,/ What a punishment new/ Shall be found out for you,/ Who, tasting, have robbed the whole tree?[66]

Pope wrote this in 1720s England. By the 1870s in America, the entire realm of religion had become the domain and the responsibility of women.[67] Woman had not only "robbed the whole tree," she had set herself up as the guardian of it. And men loved having it so.

We wrote in the first chapter of the formal disestablishment of the Church in the 1830s and of how this led to the Church—and specifically the clergy—losing almost all of their worldly prestige. Clergymen were not courted, counseled, or valued in the halls of business or politics. As sociologist Steven Goldberg points out in his 1993 book, *Why Men Rule*, when power, prestige, and payment decline for a profession, so do the numbers of men in it. Men, who had controlled the spheres of world and church while delegating the sphere of home to women, were led by economic pride and worldly prestige to abandon their responsibility in the sphere of the Church. They did this by relegating it to the same sphere as the home. The sphere of the Church was left to the women.

This had the effect of privatizing morality and religion. God was tucked safely away in the home with the women, and men were allowed to run the world any way they pleased.

Unlike many men, women, for the most part, did not leave the Church when it was disestablished. They remained and became, in effect, the minister's support group. Professor Ann Douglas observed in her 1977 book, *The Feminization of American Culture*, that, "the nineteenth-century minister moved in a world of women. He preached mainly to women; he administered what sacraments he performed largely for women; he worked not only for them but with them, in mission and charity works of all kinds."[68]

But nineteenth century clergymen saw trouble brewing. They believed that although women were agitating for political rights, they, "had more chance of capturing the Church than the Senate." Women fought and won the right to enter and organize mission work, "over repeated and widespread clerical objection."[69] However, the nineteenth century clergyman was doomed as soon as he gave up the Biblical high ground and conceded that women were by nature closer to God and/or more spiritual than men. But he was led to such conclusions by his own theological errors, i.e., his own sinful weaknesses.

Consider the error of Quakerism. Believing that God spoke directly to people, men found themselves dutifully listening to more and more revelations from God through not only the mouths but the hearts of women. It has already been noted how Quakerism was a driving force behind feminism. Feminist Nancy Cott seconds this observation, saying that Quakerism, as well as the more antinomian forms of Protestant Christianity, "inspired some of the most eloquent and powerful nineteenth-century spokeswomen for equal rights and freedoms."[70]

Calvinism also opened the doors to female leadership. Calvinism dominated the eighteenth century church scene in America. Reaction to Calvinism dominated the nineteenth.

Protestant clergymen, reacting to the unrelenting, cold, absolute doctrine of double predestination which left people searching for certainty of salvation, pointed followers to their emotions. This reaction sentimentalized Christianity. Sweet, flowery sentiments became typical of nineteenth century Christianity. (One only has to look at the lyrics and tunes of popular hymns in this era to see this.) This emphasis on emotions appealed strongly to women who were adjusting to their newly-acquired sphere. Women were, and are, more open and better at expressing their sentiments than men, so many Protestant clergymen found themselves listening to women who had heretofore been silent.

In particular, Revivalism spread this practice. The famous Finney revivals of the mid-nineteenth century regularly called on both men and women to pray aloud. "This marked a radical break with the practice of a lot of people who, up to this point, had taken the instruction of St. Paul for women to be quiet in the church quite literally."[71] It is ironic that the present heirs of Finney, from the charismatic movement to the Promise Keepers organization are so adamant in asserting the spiritual leadership of men in the home and church when their theology helped drive them out in the first place.

Men gave the spiritual headship entrusted to them over to women; they made religion "a woman thing." But when the head of a thing is changed, you necessarily change the thing itself. This transformation can best be illustrated by the portraiture of angels in the nineteenth century. Although all the pronouns referring to angels in Scripture are masculine, pictures of angels painted in the nineteenth century are not only feminine but actual females!

The transformation did not stop with angels—God was transformed also. Nineteenth century novelist Herman Melville complained in *Moby Dick* about a "soft, curled, hermaphroditical" Christ. A nineteenth century congregationalist preacher complained, "The Sword of the Spirit [is]...so muffled up and decked out with flowers and ribbons as no longer to show what it is."[72]

As God, Christ, church, and religion became more feminized, more and more men shied away from them and, in particular, from the ministry. The soft, sensitive, more feminized males were the ones that people usually directed (and still do) towards the ministry. This, in turn, only continued and escalated the feminization process because then even more men were pushed away from the Church. Then, of course, women must become pastors because there are so few men who are willing. Paganism has always had a female clergy because they have also always had a female god. Visible Christianity will end up having a female god just like paganism if it continues to accept women clergy.

If men do not boldly stand up and declare unequivocally that Christianity is not about feelings, life cycles, and relationships, but about Father, Son, and Holy Spirit, we will not only end up with a feminized church but a paganized one. Christianity is a linear religion: it is about Him who knows where He came from and where He is going to. It is about the One, who for the joy set before Him, endured the cross on the way there. The nature religions, the fertility religions, the pagan religions, and all of witchcraft are cyclical faiths.[73] From these comes such things as "death is a part of life," "holistic" thinking, and the feminine cycle of maiden, mother, crone.[74] From these things come the relativistic understanding that destinations do not matter; only journeys do.

All of paganism sees life as some type of never-ending cycle with no ultimate point. Christianity sees life as hurtling towards a day, already set, when God will judge the world by the Man, Jesus Christ. Paganism can be soft, accepting, easygoing because it lacks any ultimate goal or point of reference. Christianity calls to urgency, decisiveness and the restraint of feelings because it has an ultimate goal and point of reference. Therefore, there is only *one* thing needful, and nothing in the world, not even the whole world itself, is worth losing that one thing. For the sake of this one thing, though men are very weak, they pray to be decisive, urgent, and strong through Christ.

It is manifest, though, that men have not been these things. They have not only given up their spiritual headship, but they have given up that part of headship which they are naturally fit for even after the Fall. They have given up their physical headship. Able-bodied men sit safely in homes while smaller, weaker women police the streets and the majority of Americans do not think anything is wrong with this.

"Hold on there. I have known women who are stronger, braver, and more capable than most men." And that has been the situation in every age; exceptional women can always be found. (Although none are an exception in terms of their relative importance over against men in the reproduction of life.) Writing of London 1756-1789, Will and Ariel Durant said, "Some women tried to be men, and almost succeeded; we hear of cases where women disguised themselves as men and maintained the deception till death; some joined the army or navy as men, drank, smoked, and swore like men, fought in battle, and bore flogging manfully."[75]

Of course, such women are the heros of feminism, the mainstays of courses in the women's studies department, the shockers that are used to jolt men or women who dare even intimate that there are some things women ought not to do. But, as always, the exceptions prove the validity of the rule; if there were not accepted roles, duties, places for men and women, if there was not some created order shaping how everyone looks at males and females, the description of the Durants of women who "tried to be men" and did things "like" and "as" men and even "manfully" would be meaningless. They can only write what they do because there are rules and therefore exceptions. These "exceptional" women can still shock us even today precisely because even over thirty years of intense feminization cannot drive God's created order entirely out of our system.

We do not deny that there have been (and still are) circumstances where women needed to work like men. But historically when this did occur, women still only worked *like* men. That is, they did work like a man but always as a woman. Women did men's work the way a woman would do it, not the way a man would. For example, women were a part of the industrial revolution from the beginning. They were in the factories and the shops right alongside men, but their relationship to industry has always been different than that of men. "From the outset women's employment was shaped around the family, while man's work, in a real sense shaped the family."[76]

Distinctions were found in the agricultural sector, too. Women on the farm did much of the work in the nineteenth and early twentieth century, but there was a division, a sharp division, according to gender. A Montana man's words written in the 1880s express the then-prevailing view: "A woman is queen in her own home, but we neither want her as black-smith, ploughwoman, a soldier, a lawyer, a doctor, nor any such professions or handicrafts."[77] Personal diaries of pioneer women document that although women on the frontier had to do very masculine work during the initial phases of establishing a homestead, they went back willingly to a situation like that described by the man from Montana.

Men have been equipped by God to be the natural defenders of women. Surely the Holy Spirit means to give us some indication of what is expected of men and women when He calls on women to have a gentle and quiet spirit while exhorting men to courage and aggressiveness.[78] Surely God is telling us something, preaching a sermon to us in our very bodies, by truisms such as these: men are taller, stronger, more aggressive, and have more stamina than women. It would not be true, let alone a truism, to say *all* men are taller, stronger, and more aggressive than *all* women; but overall, men are these things compared to women.

Surely our God must be preaching to us a sermon of sorts by having the male more expendable (population-wise) than the female. Old timers in Texas would say when several male babies in a row were born in the parish that God was preparing us for war. While such reasoning is dubious, it is significant that people know that men are more expendable than women, both numerically and practically. People have always known that population levels are not greatly affected by men dying, but they are radically effected by a corresponding number of women dying. And while neither is a nice thing to see, something deep inside of us says it is more of a tragedy to see a motherless family than a fatherless one.

Without exception, societies all around the world have recognized that men should protect and lead women. This can be proven by the fact that every culture known to have existed has raised their men this way. This is the conclusion of Steven Goldberg, a recognized, secular, sociological authority. Men in every society (and he studied them all, particularly those that were suppose to be different) are socialized to be the dominant protectors. At this point the feminist will cry "foul," saying that it is not that men are better equipped for that role but that they are socialized for it. Goldberg defends his own conclusions saying, "The argument that males exhibit dominance behavior because they are socialized to do so merely begs the question: Why is it males in every society who are so socialized?"[79]

Sociology cannot answer this question; neither can evolution. Creation can. Societies have merely followed the pattern which God laid out for them in creating males with greater strength, more lung capacity, larger hearts, and bigger frames. Even fallen societies with a mere modicum of common sense can look at the average man and woman and choose which one they would rather have manning the defenses!

Of course, modern men and women will say, "It does not take a two hundred pound man to push a button." Two responses are in order. First, all combat will eventually come down to soldiers or police officers on the ground physically holding positions. No matter how much technology or fire power a country or a city has, to establish or keep a peace, troops (soldiers or police) will have to be physically present. Second, even if it is a matter of button pushing, button pushers still die in war and police actions. Losing a two hundred pound man is tragic, but losing a wife, a mother, a woman to save a two hundred pound man is foolishly tragic. No matter how many two hundred pound men we save none will ever bear a baby or babies to make up for the women lost.

God equipped men naturally for dominance, leadership, and defense. He also called upon men to sacrifice for women and children. This is implicit in the fact that God punishes so sharply those who take advantage of women and children—particularly those without the full benefit of male protection: widows and orphans. It is explicit in Ephesians 5 where God says that a husband is to be willing to sacrifice his life for his wife. This is the test of a man's love: not whether he is romantic, talkative, or spends a lot of time with his wife, but will he die for her? All of this is so deeply ingrained in us that even the person who has never heard of Ephesians has a sense of it. Husbands are to be willing to die for their wives. That is fitting. By the same token, it does not seem at all fitting for a wife to die for her husband. But it does indeed "fit" for a mother to die for her child. And so we are back to the wonderful God-given order of things.

But men have messed up the order terribly by abdicating their role. In their gross sinfulness they have allowed women to lead, defend, dominate, and not only to sacrifice for them, but men have sacrificed them! They have followed Abraham who thought nothing of sacrificing his wife's virtue and modesty to protect his life. They have followed Barek, who, though called by God to do so, would not rise to the defense of Israel unless Deborah went with him. They have followed the pusillanimous King Ahab who pouted over childish things while his wife led him.

Today women are sacrificed by men in the work force. A female social scientist of the 1920s made this observation. "As our pleasure philosophy takes deeper hold, as the demand for luxuries, artificially stimulated by advertising, mounts giddily higher, there is no help for it—the women have to go to work."[80] This is exactly what happened, but where have the luxuries ended up? Not in the laps of the women, at least not the "big ticket" items. A woman may have nicer clothes, jewelry, and furniture because she works outside of the home. But the "toys," the true luxuries—the boats, the guns, the four wheelers, the fancy cars and trucks—go to the men so much so that women are not even said to have their "toys." That expression is reserved for the things men have, not the things belonging to women.

Women do not seem to have benefitted appreciably by going to work in droves outside of the home. Not only have the "toys" not come their way, but (as study after study has shown and as every wife knows) their increased workload outside of the home has not been coupled with a corresponding decrease of work inside of it. This historic sphere of women is still their responsibility, for the most part. Men are still very much leading and dominating, but they are taking women down the path that leads to their toy box.

God help us men; Lord deliver us men, if we ever get used to women defending us and sacrificing themselves for our sakes! If we get used to it, we will be like the dog who once tasting chicken blood becomes a chicken-eating dog going for one after another just for the taste. Men who tolerate women defending them and sacrificing themselves for them will be lead inexorably to sacrificing women. Then we will really be back to paganism where the village elders got together to throw a woman down a volcano. Paganism sacrifices its women and children (think of Molech) for the *benefit* of men; Christianity protects and defends them at the *cost* of men. But currently the most Christianized country in the world, America, has a taste for women, so the blood of women is being spilled on battlefields, is flowing in abortion clinics, and is dripping on police uniforms.

Historically, the average man did not go to war to defend such high and noble things as his president, his flag, or even his country; he might have gone to war to defend his way of life. But, more often than not, he went to war so his wife, his mother, his sister, and his daughter did not have to. A Confederate chaplain reports these words from Confederate soldiers: "Yes we will suffer and die, if need be, in defense of such noble women." "If it was not for the ladies, God bless them, there would be no use fighting this war."[81]

What has happened to make men applaud and advocate women going to war in our police forces, if not in our armies? Are we so jaded that we are not bothered by the suffering of women at our expense? Or are we so "Americanized" that since this is a free country and women want to defend us we think they ought to have the right to do so? (This was the argument, by the way, of those who wanted to work women and children half to death in the sweatshops of the nineteenth century.)

The Israelis experimented with women in combat. The experience of women captured in 1948 showed them the unspeakable tortures their women would endure when captured. They were not able to tolerate this, so they passed laws requiring women to be evacuated from the front if hostilities break out.[82]—a nation which denies Christ and Christianity has nobler laws than a nation which has Christianity as a part of her cornerstone.

General Patton is famous for saying that no soldier ever won a war by dying for his country; he won by making the other guy die for his. Not only do we not win as a nation if men allow (or even make) women die for them, but men themselves lose. Judith Stiehm, a feminist, saw this. She said, "If women were to enter combat, men would lose a crucial identity which is uniquely theirs, a role which has been as male-defining as child-bearing has been female defining."[83]

Because of feminism, many women have lost their definition as women. Women without definition become depressed, but they are still human; men without definition become animals. When men lose what is male-defining, they do what is unmasculine: they persecute and sacrifice women. Consider the rape statistics of various countries. The rape rate in the United States is about seven times higher than Europe's average. Countries that are far more patriarchal than the United States (e.g., Greece, Portugal, and Japan) have a rape rate many times lower than ours.[84] It has not always been this way. In the 1830s, the French sociologist Alexis de Tocqueville observed that in France rape was only punished lightly and conviction was difficult. In the United States, he noted, rape was one of the capital offenses still remaining.[85] Now a good rape scene in a movie assures a good box office draw and even more video rentals. American men have become chicken-eating dogs.

This weakness of men drives women towards feminist ideals and viewpoints. As men stand by allowing and even advocating that women defend them and sacrifice for them, the suffering of women mounts. So women feel compelled to defend themselves because they do not trust themselves to the care of men. Men, in turn, respond by saying, "Then go ahead and do it yourself." And so men get even more comfortable with the idea of women defending and sacrificing for them.

The cycle is an ugly, vicious one. It will only lead to more dead women and more demoralized men which will lead to even more dead women and eventually totally depraved men—i.e., paganism. If Professor Richard A. Gabriel is right, it will also lead to a defeated country. "It will avail us little if the members of our defeated force are all equal. History will treat us for what we were: a social curiosity that failed."[86] In truth, we are a moral degenerate state that is failing fast.

Notes:

[1] Will Durant, *Our Oriental Heritage*, (New York: MJF Books, 1963) 247.

[2] Steichen, *Ungodly Rage*, (San Francisco: Ignatius Press, 1991) 381.

[3] *The Feminist Papers*, ed. Alice S. Rossi, (Boston: Northeastern University Press, 1973) 85.

[4] Goldberg, *Why Men Rule*, (Chicago: Open Court, 1993) 74.

[5] AE 9: 224

[6] AE 4: 290.

[7] Will and Ariel Durant, *Rousseau and Revolution*, (New York: MJF Books, 1967) 731.

[8] *The Feminist Papers*, 580.

[9] Nicene and Post-Nicene Fathers, ed. Philip Schaff, vol. 7, (Edinburgh: T&T Clark, 1988) 339.

[10] Stephen B. Clark, *Man and Woman in Christ*, (Ann Arbor; Servant Books, 1980) 291.

[11] Elliot, *Let Me Be A Woman*, (Wheaton: Tyndale House Publishers, 1976) 122-123.

[12] Oddie, *What Will Happen To God?*, (San Francisco: Ignatius Press, 1988) 54.

[13] Nicene and Post-Nicene Fathers, vol. 12, 150.

[14] *The Feminist Papers*, 11.

[15] Hardenbrook, 34.

[16] Frank G. Slaughter, *The Stubborn Heart*, (Garden City: Doubleday, 1950) 221.

[17] Degler, *At Odds*, (New York: Oxford University Press, 1980) 175.

[18] Christian News, Herman Otten, ed., 12-2-85, 3.

[19] Steichen, n.109, 321.

[20] Friedan, *The Feminine Mystique*, (New York: Dell Publishing, 1983) 95.

[21] Degler, 348.

[22] Will and Ariel Durant, *The Age of Voltaire*, (New York: MJF Books, 1965) 84.

[23] Gilder, *Men and Marriage*, (Gretna: Pelican Publishing, 1986) 5.

[24] John Eidsmoe, *Christianity and the Constitution*, (Grand Rapids: Baker Book House, 1987) 272.

[25] *The Feminist Papers*, 563.

[26] Friedan, 77.

[27] *The Feminist Papers*, 675.

[28] AE 51, 88.

[29] Belonick, 45.

[30] *The Age of Voltaire*, 65.

[31] *The Feminist Papers*, 682.

[32] ibid., 675.

[33] Green, *The Light of the Home*, (New York: Panethon Books, 1983) 116.

[34] Degler, 381.

[35] The Feminist Papers, 357.

[36] Cott, *The Grounding of Feminism*, (New Haven: Yale University Press, 1987) 228.

[37] Clark, 410.

[38] Cott, 20.

[39] Martin Luther, *Luther's Works*, ed. Jaroslav Pelikan, vol. 4, "Lectures on Genesis," trans. George Schick, (St. Louis: Concordia, 1964) 302.

[40] Noah Smithwick, *The Evolution of a State or Recollections of Old Texas Days*, (Austin: University of Texas Press, 1983) 5.

[41] Douglas, *The Feminization of American Culture*, (New York: Alfred A. Knopf, 1977) 194.

[42] Friedan, 90.

[43] Green, 115.

[44] Degler, 354.

[45] Green, 131.

[46] Carl A. Volz, *Pastoral Life and Practice in the Early Church*, (Minneapolis: Augsburg, 1990) 148-149.

[47] Green, 143.

[48] ibid., 122.

[49] ibid., 143, 122.

[50] *The Feminist Papers*, 50.

[51] ibid., 10-11.

[52] ibid., 467.

[53] Elliot, *Let Me Be a Woman*, 143.

[54] Cott, 111.

[55] Barry Asmus, "Points to Ponder," *Reader's Digest*, March 1996, 31.

[56] The Nicene and Post-Nicene Fathers, ed. Philip Schaff, vol. 12, (Grand Rapids: Eerdmans, 1983) 97.

[57] Steichen, 381.

[58] Nicene and Post-Nicene Fathers, vol. vii, 222.

[59] Helen Hitchcock in Steichen, 11.

[60] Kassian, *The Feminist Gospel*, (Wheaton: Crossway Books, 1992) 106.

[61] Sommers, *Who Stole Feminism?*, (New York: Simon & Schuster, 1994) 33.

[62] ibid., 65.

[63] ibid., 91.

[64] ibid.

[65] Belonick, 21.

[66] Will and Ariel Durant, *Voltaire*, 207.

[67] Green, 173.

[68] Douglas, 97.

132

[69] Douglas, 110, 111.

[70] Cott, 17.

[71] Hardenbrook, 58.

[72] Douglas, 113.

[73] Steichen, 34.

[74] ibid., 85.

[75] *Rousseau and Revolution*, 731.

[76] Degler, 395.

[77] Degler, 408.

[78] Clark, 633.

[79] Goldberg, 103.

[80] Cott, 184.

[81] William W. Bennett, *The Great Revival in the Southern Armies*, (Harrisonburg: Sprinkle Publications, 1989) 62, 50-51.

[82] Brian Mitchell, Weak Link: *The Feminization of the American Military*, (Washington, D.C.: Regnery Gateway, 1989) 206.

[83] Mitchell, 218.

[84] Sommers, 223.

[85] Tocqueville, vol. 2, 213-214.

[86] Mitchell, 216.

CHAPTER IV
THE FEMININE MISTAKE

F eminism has progressed unabated now for thirty years in large part because it appeals to the feminine *mistake*. This is not to be confused with feminine *mystique*. Betty Friedan launched the modern era of feminism with her 1963 book, *The Feminine Mystique*. She explains the term in that work: "There was a strange discrepancy between the reality of our lives as women and the image to which we were trying to conform, the image that I came to call the feminine mystique."[1]

The phrase "feminine *mistake*" does not refer to that; the feminine mistake is simply that women are inherently dissatisfied, and they allow their dissatisfaction to rule them to the point where they will tear down their own houses with their very own hands. This should not seem strange to Scripture-taught Christians. Satan succeeded in making Eve dissatisfied in a perfect paradise. She, in turn, shared her dissatisfaction with her husband by sharing the fruit forbidden to them. As a result, she was cursed so that her insatiable desire would always be towards her husband; she would have a never ending desire in that direction.

The Bible clearly sees this tendency in fallen women. The Book of Proverbs speaks only of a nagging woman, never a nagging man. A nagging woman is, of course, a dissatisfied one. Feminists will quickly retort, "The Bible speaks only of nagging women because men wrote the Bible!" The redeemed in Christ do not have this 'out'; we must deal with passages such as these: "Better live on the corner of a roof than share a home with a quarreling woman" (Pr. 21:9). "A constant dripping on a rainy day and a nagging wife are alike" (Pr. 27:15).

"Better to live in a desert than with a quarreling and nagging woman" (Pr. 21:19). And it is the woman, not the man, who is warned of the foolishness of tearing down one's own home: "Every wise woman builds her house: but the foolish tear it down with her hands" (Pr. 14:1).

God "preaches" to women what their roles are to be by their biology, in particular, and by sociology, in general. In addition, He tells them where their satisfaction is to be found. He tells them they are to "stand under" their husbands, bear children, be in charge of their homes, and be lovers of both husbands and children. (See Eph. 5, I Tim. 2, and Titus 2.)

The Lutheran *Apology to the Augsburg Confession* shows how these roles are really oriented towards the woman's eternal salvation, commenting on St. Paul's startling statement in I Timothy 2:15, "she shall be saved in childbearing":

> Paul says that woman is saved through bearing children. In contrast to the hypocrisy of celibacy, what greater honor could he bestow than to say that woman is saved by the marital functions themselves, by marital intercourse, by childbirth, and by her domestic duties. (XXIII, 32)

This sounds almost surrealistic to our feminized ears. But the fact is that none of the 'second wave' feminists, the nineteenth century ones, ever argued that woman should cease being the primary rearers as well as the bearers of children.[2] Even so, Ida Tarbell, a female historian and journalist writing at the beginning of the twentieth century, notes that what kept women in the 1840s away from the women's rights movement was a fear that they would destroy their lives as wives and mothers.[3]

At one time, women were satisfied with their roles of wife and mother. These roles were not something forced on them in the Dark Ages; a 1990s secular sociologist asserts that psychologically and physiologically modern women will only find satisfaction in connection with their roles of wife and mother.

I believe that the evidence indicates that women follow their own psychophysiological imperatives and that they would not choose to compete for the goals that men devote their lives to attaining. Women have more important things to do. Men are aware of this and that is why in this and in every other society they look to women for gentleness, kindness, and love, for refuge from a world of pain and force, for safety from their own excesses. In every society a basic male motivation is the feeling that the women and children must be protected. But a woman cannot have it both ways: if she wishes to sacrifice all this, what she will get in return is the right to meet men on male terms. She will lose.[4]

Goldberg asserts that women will lose if they are not satisfied with their roles; the Christian (who believes those roles to be God-given) knows the loss can be potentially catastrophic. To not be satisfied with what God has given is to not be satisfied with God. To seek a glory that God has not given is to eclipse the glory He has given. St. Chrysostom, writing over 1,500 years ago, explains in a homily on I Corinthians:

> But if any say, 'Nay, how can this be a shame to the woman if she mount up to the glory of the man?' We might make the answer; 'She doth not mount up, but rather falls from her own proper honor.' Since not to abide within our own limits and the laws ordained of God, but to go beyond, is not an addition but a diminution....[T]he woman acquireth not the man's dignity but loseth even the woman's decency which she had. And not from hence only is her shame and reproach, but also on account of her covetousness.[5]

Covetousness is a desire that can never be legitimately satisfied. Men have the sinful tendency to covet what they do not have in the way of women and money. Women have a sinful tendency to covet whatever they think they need to be happy. Men chase objects more than feelings; women do the opposite.

Coveting is never good, but it is particularly destructive when you covet to be something or someone else. Tragically, women have been brought to the point of believing that they need to cast off womanhood in order to be happy, fulfilled, etc. Soren Kierkegaard said it first and Simon de Beauvoir quoted him in her 1949 book, *The Second Sex*: "[W]hat a misfortune it is to be a woman! And yet the greatest misfortune when one is a woman is not to realize that it is one."[6]

No, there is a much greater misfortune: it is to be a woman but not comprehend what a privilege, honor, blessing, and glory it is to be one. Scripture says that the woman is the glory of the man (I Corinthians 11:7), not, as Kierkegaard and Beauvoir seem to think, that man is the glory of the woman! Our Lord Jesus Christ became incarnate not in the womb of a woman, and He deigned from Creation on that it be through women that all men come into the world, even though the first woman came through a man in His order of Creation.

Christian "philosopher" G.K. Chesterton also reached different conclusions from those of the negative Kierkegaard and Beauvoir.

> Now when society is in a rather futile fuss about the subjection of women, will no one say how much every man owes to the tyranny and privilege of women, to the fact that they alone rule education until education becomes futile: for a boy is only sent to be taught at school when it is too late to teach him anything. The real thing has been done already, and thank God it is nearly always done by women. Every man is woman-ized, merely by being born.[7]

What can be done if a woman is not satisfied with her gender? Goldberg delineates that this is truly a curse:

Sex is the single most decisive determinant of personal identity; it is the first thing we notice about another person and the last thing we forget. Just as it is criminal for others to limit one's identity by invoking arbitrary limitations in the name of nature, so it is terribly self-destructive to refuse to accept one's own nature and the joys and powers it invests.[8]

What could have led women to such a terrible self-rejection of their gender? What could have led them to being dissatisfied at such a basic level? We saw that the seed of dissatisfaction was planted by Satan and that insatiability became a part of the curse that women have borne ever since. But what led women to the point of bluntly rejecting womanhood?

"Women had it bad before the advent of the women's rights movement." That is the standard answer, but the evidence suggests otherwise. Women were not the serfs of any Christian society. In Europe, around the time that women's rights became to rumble in the distance, a woman named Laura Bassi received a doctorate in philosophy at age 21; was appointed to a professorship; lectured on Newton's *Opticks*; wrote treatises on physics; gave her husband twelve children; and educated them herself.[9] Certainly this woman was an exceptional human being, but the fact that a woman in 1730 was free to pursue such things is telling.

However, the statements made by feminists and by impartial observers concerning life in America are also quite revealing. Feminist Francis Wright admitted in 1820 that in her day, "public attention is now everywhere turned to the improvement of female education."[10] Wright went on to observe in the same essay: "It strikes me that it would be impossible for women to stand in higher estimation than they do here [in America]....In domestic life there is a tenderness on the part of the husband to his weaker helpmate, and this in all situations of life that I believe in no country is surpassed and in few equaled."[11]

Tocqueville, the French observer and chronicler of American society in the 1830s, not only noted that men and women had separate spheres in America, he defended it because (in his opinion) it reflected mutual respect between husband and wife. He said that Americans did not believe that two sexes should have the same roles, "but they show an equal regard for both their respective parts; and though their lot is different, they consider both of them as beings of equal value."[12]

Writing in the 1980s, feminist Nancy Cott testifies to the tremendous "advances" women made in the 1920s. "Women maturing in the 1920s had been accustomed during their whole youthful lives to hearing news of women's advance in the labor force and in the public arena."[13] Throughout the '90s, both male and female social commentators have made similar observations. Even while Betty Friedan was sounding the call to arms for the plight of the American women, anthropologist Dr. William Stephens was saying in 1963, "If there are any exceptional societies (in which each family may freely choose - or fight it out - to determine who does what), our own society probably comes as close as any....In the allocation of power and privilege our society - compared with other societies - treats wives most generously."[14]

Feminists will respond to Stephens' remarks by saying that they only prove how bad the subjection was at the time. The man, Stephens, could rejoice in the stations of men and women, while women (until Friedan came along) suffered in silence. But Stephens' remarks help explain what puzzled even Friedan at the time: she noted that while women comprised about 50 percent of the nation's professionals in 1930, by 1960 their percentage had dropped to 35 percent, despite the fact that the number of female college graduates almost tripled during this thirty year time frame. "The phenomenon was the great increase in the numbers of educated women choosing to be just housewives."[15] This is not a "phenomenon" at all if, as Stephens claimed, Americans ca. 1960 treated wives more generously than any other society on earth.

Nevertheless, things changed radically for women in the 1970s. Up until then, as incredible as it may sound, the occupational patterns of women had not changed since 1800.[16] But things changed dramatically beginning around 1970: women entered the work force in ever-increasing numbers; they cut their children loose from their apron strings at the same time as they cut them loose from their umbilical cords, placing them in day care at ever-earlier ages; and they began having large amounts of personal disposable income.

No one could argue with the statement that from 1970 on women were free (or at least more free) to fully develop their strength and beauty as women then ever before. Margaret Fuller said in 1848 that if women were allowed to do just that they would not wish to assume what belonged to men; they would be satisfied with what was theirs; in other words, they would not have that unquenchable desire for the place of men. She said, "[T]he only reason why women ever assume what is more appropriate to you [men], is because you prevent them from finding out what is fit for themselves. Were they free, were they wise fully to develop the strength and beauty of woman, they would never wish to be men."[17]

Well, women have come a very long way; they have achieved exactly what the more moderate feminists of the late-nineteenth and early-twentieth century wanted. And yet, are they satisfied? No, not if you believe the polls, women's magazines, and the legions of therapists treating women for depression. Women are as depressed, downtrodden, demoralized, and dehumanized as ever before, probably more so. Could it be that women will never be satisfied? I think so. Illegitimate desires can never be satisfied; that is one of their marks. A woman's desire for the place of the man is illegitimate—it will forever be unfulfilled. Goldberg agrees: he says that some women (the author would say "all," based on the Fall and resulting curse) have an insatiable desire that males no longer dominate.[18] The feminine mistake is the attempt to build a life around a desire that can never be satisfied.

Of course, unsatisfiable desires are something that every Christian, male or female, must struggle against. Christian men must fight against the insatiable desire to love many women and instead freely love the one wife to which God has joined them. Christian women are called upon by Christ to fight against the insatiable desire for the place of the man by freely standing under the husband Christ has given them.

But the struggle in which Christian women are engaged is being sabotaged. What if there was an entire industry whose one mission was to entice a man away from his wife? There is, you say; it is called pornography. But society protects and insulates men from this industry in some measure through social mores and even, in some cases, by laws. Women have no such protection against the industry that lays in ambush for them. The industry that entices them to constant dissatisfaction is legal, and it is absolutely ubiquitous in modern culture. It is called advertising.

Seventy-five percent of all consumer advertising budgets are spent appealing to women; this was observed not in 1993 (after women had been "emancipated" to earn those big paychecks and had more say in how money was spent), but by Betty Friedan in 1963.[19] Already in the 1920s, during the toddling years of the industry, advertising experts said that women made 80 percent of consumer purchases. Feminist Nancy Cott says the modern advertising industry was born in the 1920s, and from its birth most ads were beamed directly at women. Cott references a 1929 advertising journal: "As one ad in the industry journal put it, 'The proper study of mankind is *man*...but the proper study of markets is *woman*.'"[20]

The fact that women are more susceptible to advertising than men are is a viewpoint that goes back to the nineteenth century and forward with us into the twenty-first. Nathaniel Fowler, "the most important figure in early American advertising," said in the nineteenth century that, "an advertisement has not one twentieth the weight with a man that it has with a woman of equal intelligence and the same social status..."[21] An advertising industry now at the dawn of a new century knows this, as well; it knows that women are more fickle in the marketplace then men. Ads today are aimed at women's "softer focus" and they stress "gauzy emotional appeals over hard, rational argument."[22] Perhaps this has something to do with the universally admitted fact that men insist on controlling the television remote and habitually flip through commercials!

Feminists readily admit that women are more influenced by advertising than men. Friedan believes that women were never allowed to be what they really wanted to be but were always chasing after the image which advertisers dangled before them. But, ironically, Friedan is not so concerned with the fact that women chase after such images but with *which* image they are chasing. When Friedan entered the magazine field ca. 1960 she was told by a magazine editor (a woman herself) that the old image of the spirited career girl which flourished from about 1939 to 1949 was largely created by writers and editors who were women. The new image of the woman as the housewife and mother which was popular from about 1949 to 1959 was largely the creation of writers and editors who were men. According to that female magazine editor, the change happened in this way: during World War II there were no men to write, so women who carried the responsibility at home and office did the writing. They wrote in the spirit of the day in which they lived. When the men returned home, they displaced the women writers and wrote of the cozy warm housewives and mothers they had been dreaming of while overseas.[23]

This explanation seems plausible enough, but it does not address the fact that, according to Friedan's own understanding, women look to magazine articles and advertisements (regardless of whether such are produced by men or women), for their role models and to determine who they should be. Friedan returns repeatedly to the theme that women are so unsure of who they are, "that they look to this glossy public image to decide every detail of their lives."[24] But she never deals with the inherent dissatisfaction bubbling forth from women which advertisers capitalize on and to which advertisements appeal. She tries to blame this ever-present dissatisfaction on the fact that modern women were raised by mothers who were miserable. All women could know from such rearing was that they did not want to be like the mothers who raised them, but they could not have known what else they could be.

But this view conflicts with what Friedan asserts concerning women leaving the work force behind after World War II in large numbers, choosing instead to be wives and mothers. She asks in amazement, "Not long ago women dreamed and fought for equality, their own place in the world. What happened to their dreams, when did women decide to give up the world and go back home?"[25] And her explanation that women of the '60s did not know what they should be because they were raised by mothers miserable in motherhood does not explain why after 25 years of "be anything you want to be," advertisers are still certain they can dangle images before women and women will chase them. The inherent dissatisfaction found in women is not caused by advertisers or the plight of miserable women: women are miserable because they are inherently afflicted with dissatisfaction from the Fall on; advertisers simply take advantage of this dissatisfaction.

Nancy Cott, writing some twenty-four years after Friedan, picks up on this theme of advertising. She sees "modern merchandising as co-opting the feminists movement by taking the feminist dictum that women needed to take control over their own lives and translating it into 'the consumerist notion of choice.'"[26] By referencing scientific studies, advertising gained credibility with women and so won the upper hand when it came to prescribing models for women to be fulfilled. Whereas the Church and/or the State controlled the lives of women with their concept of duty, popular media and advertising replaced it with personal adjustment and fulfillment. Cott believes that advertising caused things to be "demanded from within" from women, thereby enslaving them worse than church or state ever did.[27]

Our thesis is that feminism was not co-opted by merchandising; rather, feminism co-opted the merchandising mentality. It continually dangled a "carrot" (or, more accurately, some forbidden fruit) before women. Feminism has always appealed to women by playing to the weakness of dissatisfaction that it knew women had from the Fall on. Merchandising appeals to the same thing, but feminism predates the advertising industry by over fifty years.

Moreover, Cott's thesis does not explain why advertisement has not done a similar thing to men. Why have men not learned to demand things from within the way women have? The author's thesis explains the difference. Men's inherent weakness is not dissatisfaction; it is following women, and they are doing so in the area of advertising even as Adam first did it in the Garden. More and more, men are evaluating their lives and their happiness based on a standard given to them by the advertising industry: I am miserable or less than happy because I lack this brand or do not look this way. So, in a very real way, far from merchandising co-opting feminism for its purposes (as Cott believes) feminism has succeeded in co-opting merchandising for its own purposes. Feminism used mass media and advertising successfully for its own ends. It has used them to spread its message of dissatisfaction to women and men in all walks of life.

But before feminism could co-opt advertising methodology, individual woman were co-opted by their own intrinsic dissatisfaction. Alice S. Rossi, the editor of one of the cardinal texts of feminism, *The Feminist Papers*, gives this account of Elizabeth Cady Stanton's admission of being influenced by

144

Susan B. Antony:

> Thirty years later, when Elizabeth was no longer
> burdened with housekeeping and child-rearing re-
> sponsibilities, she commented that in the 1850s, had
> it not been for Susan, who provided her with enough
> evidence of injustice 'to turn any woman's thoughts
> from stockings and puddings,' she might in time, 'like
> too many women, have become wholly absorbed in a
> narrow family selfishness.'[28]

One must wonder whether the injustices done to women were really so glaring if one had to "sell" the concept to another to make her discontent with her home life. But even Friedan admits that she needed to be "sold" the idea that there was indeed a problem, but the "sale" was made *by* herself *to* herself. She says, while looking back on the writing of her landmark book, "It is a decade now since the publication of *The Feminine Mystique*, and until I started writing the book, I wasn't even conscious of the women problem."[29]

Once a few women were converted to the notion that there was no satisfaction for women in husband, home, or family, feminism pedaled, sold, and advertised this notion relentlessly. An astute observer of this phenomenon said in the late 1960s, "Often these [dissatisfactions] did not reach the conscious level, especially a few generations ago, but today the question is posed by every women's magazine, 'Is your marriage a success?'"[30] Men's magazines did not do this, and it was not because men were not concerned with their marriages but because men were not as susceptible to this sort of "selling." The equivalent for men would have been magazine articles asking, "Is your wife's body sexy to you?" But everyone would have recognized such articles as being in poor taste.

The selling of feminism worked, but not right away; it worked only after the advertising industry really got "off the ground." In the 1920s, just prior to that happening, the selling of feminism had not progressed very far, despite the fact that it had been a movement for seventy years. This failure can be seen in two surveys. In 1924, three hundred and fifty high school girls were polled. When given a choice between a career and a domestic life, two-thirds chose the latter. In 1926, five hundred women were surveyed by the YMCA. Seventy-five percent believed "a woman will find her truest self-expression through her husband and children."[31] Contrast these results with those found in a survey taken after about fifty years of feminist advertising. The woman's magazine *Redbook* did a survey in 1973. Less than two percent of the women surveyed believed that a woman could reach her full potential while only being a wife and mother only.[32] Realizing that these results could have been skewed by the survey device, the "pool" which was surveyed, and even the location in which the survey was conducted, the dramatic increase of dissatisfaction with home life is still telling.

To make matters worse, if women do not respond to the "soft" sell of feminist advertising, the feminists resort to the "hard" sell: if a woman fails to become dissatisfied with her marriage, her position, or her status, then feminists attack her. Betty Friedan says, "The adjusted, or cured ones who live without conflict or anxiety in the confined world of home have forfeited their own being; the others, the miserable frustrated ones, still have some hope."[33] This, too, is an advertising ploy, is it not? Ads typically have implicit messages such as, "You obviously do not know cars if you can be satisfied with anything less than a ..." Or, "This brand is only for the buyer who has discriminating taste." If you are not dissatisfied, there is something wrong with you. That is pretty much what Satan said to Eve.

We do not know if Satan's design here is explicitly to make women dissatisfied with home, husband, and/or family, or just to keep women in a constant state of dissatisfaction.

Feminists constantly portray women caught between the "rock" of home, family, or husband and the "hard place" of career, world, or prestige. Who could be satisfied in such a terrible squeeze? But who could choose given such terrible choices? Jessie Taft, a feminist, wrote in 1916 that modern women were faced with, "a choice between a crippled life in the home or an unfulfilled one out of it."[34] What kind of a real choice is this? It is like the experiments where a mouse is forced to choose between the smaller of two platforms. If it jumps on the larger of the two, it is shocked. A mouse does fine until the relative difference in the size of the two platforms is so close that it has no apparent choice. The mouse does not jump at all, and remains on its original platform having the equivalent of a nervous breakdown.

That women are indeed being prodded to make impossible choices can be seen from the fact that, as Friedan and other feminists have observed, women continually go back to the home, family, and husband that they allegedly want so desperately to be free of—this happened at the end of the abolition movement, at the end of the suffrage movement, and at the end of World War II. Each time they returned, there were many articles published on the plight of women who had nothing but home, husband, and family. Women are forever being knocked from pillar to post not only by unbelieving men but by women stirring the pot of dissatisfaction which bubbles underneath the fallen nature of women.

Many men dismiss the endemic disquiet of women as hormonal. Without a doubt hormones, genes and environment do come into play, but (as many scientist are now admitting) the interrelationship of these things is so complex it is impossible to be dogmatic about cause and effect relationships. Besides, a word of caution is in order here. The hormonal understanding of adolescence has only given us unruly teens who are not held accountable for their behavior and who are being catered to at every turn. We may expect a similar thing to result if we give in to a hormonal understanding of female dissatisfaction. If fact, we can already see the trend in this direction. How often do movies, talk shows, sit-coms, and jokes use premenstrual syndrome to excuse outlandish female behavior?

Father Van Ginneken has the correct outlook on this matter. Writing in the 1920s, he said that if the Church did not offer Christ to modern women, *spiritual hunger* would draw them not to just the secular women's movement, but to communism[35], the occult, spiritism, and theosophy.[36] The empty, aching need that women so frequently complain about is neither the product of neglect or mistreatment nor of hormones or genes but of the Fall. She who was beguiled by Satan to the point of being spiritually hungry in the fullness of paradise is *cursed* by God to be forever spiritually hungry in this fallen, barren world. This *curse* draws women in larger numbers than men to the Church, but it also draws them to many illegitimate means for satisfying their spiritual hunger. Women in their fallen natures always want something more, and this attracts them in large numbers to those hawking more spirituality (the Pentecostals); more peace of mind (the psychologists and psychiatrists); or more abundant life (the malls and home shopping networks).

But no fallen woman will be satisfied with her life in this fallen world, even as no fallen man will be satisfied with his wife in this fallen world. But the problem is not the woman's life or the man's wife; the problem is the fallen woman and the fallen man. But women are not being told this by feminism, by society, and (now) not even by the Church. Women are being told that their *life* is the problem, not their *desires*.

Women should not expect that their home life will be fully satisfying or totally occupying in this fallen world, yet they do.[37] And if their home life cannot be identified as the problem, then life itself becomes the problem, not the self. "The very essence of feminism," according to Crystal Eastman, writing in 1927, is "how to reconcile a woman's natural desire for love and home and children with her equally natural desire for work of her own for which she is paid."[38]

All of feminism recognizes that the tension is between self and family.[39] But the problem is not the fact that there is tension; indeed, there has always been tension at this point. The problem comes because feminism says that either men are wrong for creating the tension or women are wrong for not breaking the tension. Feminism never says that women themselves are wrong for creating the tension. Friedan at least admits that the tension comes from within: "We can no longer ignore that voice within women that says: 'I want something more than my husband and my children and my home.'"[40] Friedan even admits that this alone may be a woman's only problem. She speaks of one of the last New York analysts trained at Freud's institute in Vienna who told her that he had a woman patient on the couch for nearly two years before he could determine that her only problem was it was not enough for her to be just a housewife and a mother.[41] Freud himself evidently had trouble in this area, too. A biographer of Freud relates this remark made by the legendary psychoanalyst, "The great question that has never been answered and which I have not yet been able to answer, despite my thirty years of research into the feminine soul, is, what does a woman want?"[42] This in itself says much, but you will never hear a feminist say that a woman's dissatisfaction is *the* problem— feminists, like good revolutionaries, must feed the fires of dissatisfaction smoldering deep within every fallen woman. They must keep adding fuel to the embers of dissatisfaction glowing deep within women until a firestorm is touched off.

Literature has also noted this distinctly feminine malaise. In his *Madame Bovary*, Flaubert says of woman, "there is always some desire that draws her, some conventionality that restrains."[43] In other words, woman always finds herself between a rock and a hard place. Thomas Hardy shows the aching disquietude of women when a female character in his

Return of the Native says she, "...want[s] of an object to live for - that's all the matter with me."[44]

Friedan herself seems to be in step with these women in literature (characters admittedly created by men) when she reveals her own feminine soul. "I've always dreaded being alone more than anything else...[I]t was easier for me to start the woman's movement which was needed to change society than to change my own personal life."[45]

By telling women that their role, rather than themselves, is responsible for their unhappiness, feminists have been allowed to make caricatures of the roles of women and of the woman who willingly fills them. A caricature in words is no different than one on in pictures. Everyone knows that President Bill Clinton does not really have as big of nose, lips, and jowl as he is shown to have in the editorial cartoons. But those pictures do indeed portray *his* nose, *his* lips, *his* jowls, and by portraying them so ridiculously it makes it easier to laugh at the whole person. Likewise, feminists, playing off the dissatisfaction they themselves have created in women, have inflated, distorted, and parodied the genuine roles of women while leaving enough of the truth there for any woman to recognize her own situation and to recoil in disgust from it. But in caricaturing women's roles, feminism has also made a caricature of the God who gave those roles. Scripture does not portray women as weak, passive, and overly emotional. Scripture does not picture women as being mercilessly under the thumbs of men. Scripture does not depict women as being in an inferior position. Yet this is how feminism caricatures women and their God-given roles.

Once feminism had caricatured and rejected women's God-given roles they had to do the same thing with the God who gave them. Feminism correctly saw all the human failings that flow from fallen humanity (men's tendency to tyrannize women and women's tendency to dissatisfaction), but it rejected the doctrine of the Fall. Instead feminism blamed all of these failings on the institution of patriarchy, and that cannot be done without going back to the Patriarch of patriarchs, the eternal Father.[46] If women are not to blame for their dissatisfaction within the patriarchal way of life, then whoever created that system is to blame, as well as anyone who tells them they should be satisfied within it.

Radical feminist Mary Daly clearly saw this, and that is why she believed it was necessary to reject God's omnipotence, immutability, and providence. She correctly saw that such divine attributes only discouraged women from seeking change.[47] If God is all-powerful and unchangeable and He ordered all creation providentially, fitting it together just so, then how dare women (or men) feel justified in being dissatisfied with divinely-ordained roles?

But this tendency to go right to the source and reject God Himself did not start with the radical Mary Daly in the 1960s; the founding mothers of feminism evidenced these same tendencies. In 1895, Elizabeth Cady Stanton was so bold as to reject the God of the Bible. She said that the time had come, "to read the Bible as we do all other books, accepting the good and rejecting the evil it teaches." She felt it was important to convince women, "that Hebrew mythology had no special claim to a higher origin than that of the Greeks."[48]

Betty Friedan began *The Feminine Mystique* with the assertion that she and all other women were living a lie: "I and every other woman I knew had been living a lie, and all the doctors who treated us and the experts who studied us were perpetuating that lie, and our homes and schools and churches and politics and professions were built around that lie"[49]—the lie being that women should be satisfied with their roles as mothers, wives, and as women in God's created order. Systematically, feminism tore down homes, schools, churches, politics, and professions to build another "lie," one of their own making. The lie was that satisfaction can be found in something less than God: it can be found in the things that men have. But this is a lie because what is true of St. Augustine's soul is true of feminine souls, too: the female soul is forever restless until it finds its rest in God. Feminism asked the essentially spiritual question, "Is this all there is?" (*The Feminine Mystique* begins with this very question) and gave a totally material answer. Like Eve, women have been thoroughly deceived, beguiled, and seduced into trying to find their satisfaction in "things" and in some very surprising "things" at that.

Paradoxically two of the things that today's "liberated women" (and here we are not speaking of feminists) seek satisfaction in are the things of men, or stranger still, in satisfying men. Women seek to claw their way to the top thinking that satisfaction will be found up there where fallen men have frequently sought it. They want to be on the front lines of battle believing that there is satisfaction in dying for one's country. They want to be free to subdivide their lives between home and work believing there is satisfaction in splitting one's self. Chesterton observed 90 years ago that women have ended up believing what men never did. He said that men would go home from Parliament carrying on about how important their work was and how necessary it was to be away from home, but all the while they knew it was just talk. But the women believed what the men said, and in their dissatisfaction started longing for that sort of life, and so the public life was exalted over the private, the world over the home.[50]

Feminism and society tell women that if they do not do what men do, then they are behind men. Many a young woman is determined to push herself, despite her feelings, towards goals which others have set for them.[51] Steven Goldberg says that women who covet a state of second-rate manhood are forever condemned, "to argue against their own juices."[52]

Putting women in the situation where they feel that the only way to be accepted, have value, or *find satisfaction* is in the things of men, is the great disservice, the great discrimination that is now institutionalized in our society. It is discriminatory because men have never been told that they need to be able to do everything a woman can do; at no time have men been evaluated by feminine criteria.[53] "To subject femininity to the criteria of masculinity is as foolish as it would be to judge meat by the standards of potatoes. Meat would fail every test."[54] And so women have "failed" every test simply because they are not men! But even if they do succeed, they fail because they only succeed to the degree that they oppose themselves; to the degree that they "argue against their own juices." And even if a woman was accepted, valued, and satisfied in the things of men, it would be at the cost of denying her femininity, and "it is in their femininity that they participate in the human race."[55] As a result of being "cut-off" from their humanity, we would expect to see women plagued by depression and endlessly seeking satisfaction. This is, in fact, what we do see and have seen for decades.

There are women who seek satisfaction in the things of men: achieving and/or being valued in a man's world whether that be corporate, military or athletic. There are other women who seek satisfaction in pleasing men, in appealing to men. While they appear to be much more feminine and therefore *not* to be arguing against their own juices, this path is doomed to failure because while sinful women are never satisfied, sinful men are never satisfied with women. This is why it is women (and not men) who are on a habitual diet. It is women (not men, for the most part) who develop anorexia and bulimia. It is women (not men) who slice and dice, nip and tuck, pack and unpack, seeking satisfaction in their looks. However, such satisfaction only comes when men are pleased with their looks. And sinful men are only pleased with women as portrayed through the camera's filtered lens or on the pages of glossy magazines. Anything less does not please them as much.

This drive to be pleasing to men makes women susceptible to all sorts of advertising ploys. Women, not men, are given the goal of having their bodies fit their clothes, rather than being sold clothes that fit their body. When jeans company produced ads for loose fitting jeans, they were aimed only at men. But ads touting tight fitting jeans or jeans that shape the body are aimed at women. Earlier we noted how Victorian society developed clothing to accent certain characteristics of the female form, the breast and pelvic area particularly. Victorian women endured pinched waists, pushed up bosoms, and a pushed out buttock to satisfy not themselves but men. This trend continues into our day. Since 1939, according to Betty Friedan, women have become three and four sizes smaller.[56] The sizes did not change to fit the women; women changed to fit those sizes. The same thing happened when bikinis were the rage. Women exercised, toned, dieted, and had surgery to be able to *satisfactorily* fit the suit. They thought satisfaction would be found there. But satisfaction can never be found in satisfying men because what satisfies men is constantly changing. One year legs are "in," the next breasts will be. Blondes have more fun some years, during others they are only "stupid." The woman who needs to satisfy men in order to be satisfied will never be satisfied.

Women are on a hopeless quest if they are seeking to satisfy men with their physical appearance because women age more quickly than men do. Young women satisfy men; old women do not. A cursory glance of networks news will confirm this. Our nation will accept the withered, craggy face of David Brinkley or Walter Cronkite reporting the news and even respect them for their age. But very few women make it past fifty years old in the broadcast business. There is no way for a woman to win the age war on a man's terms.

Women, to varying degrees, escape this trap of trying to find satisfaction in pleasing unsatisfiable men, but in doing so, many fall into a secondary trap. They try to find satisfaction in children. That women are set aside by God for the privilege of bearing and nurturing children is true. That the center of their life is to be home is also true. But God never points us creatures to other created things for satisfaction. It is not only unwise to seek satisfaction there; it also quickly leads to idolatry.

Read the Book of Proverbs: how much sorrow is recorded there concerning women relative to children! Perhaps that is why the last chapter, the one containing the description of a godly mother, is introduced as "The words of King Lemuel, the oracle which his mother taught him" (Proverbs 31:1). This brief verse encourages mothers to take heart. Although so much of their mothering, as Proverbs shows, is rewarded by heartbreak, still it is not always in vain.

Mothers who do seek their satisfaction in children will always end up heartbroken either by foolish children or by an empty nest. If God intended women to find their meaning, purpose or satisfaction in children, then He would not have had their fertility run out so far ahead of their life span. Women are the only females of any species whose life span exceeds their reproductivity by thirty, forty, or more years. Feminists are partly right (which is another reason why women find them so hard to resist) when they say, "I don't want to be known just as someone's mother." Our satisfaction is not to be found in what we do or what we are but only in God; in what He is and does.

Friedan rails against the fact that for fifteen years, roughly 1945 to 1960, there was a propaganda campaign to give women prestige as housewives.[57] She may be more right than wrong in her railing. Christian books can be found that glorify washing diapers, cooking, cleaning, etc., in and of themselves. Women can and should see through that. Are women suppose to be satisfied with cleaning up vomit rather than cleaning up on the stock market? Are they suppose to be satisfied with husband and children who continually take them for granted rather than with a supervisor who will appreciate them and show it? Satisfaction is to be found in none of these things in and of themselves. But in the realm of reason, it is foolish to argue that there is more satisfaction in dishes than in dollars, in home rather than in office.

Satisfaction for women is not to be found in being men or in pleasing men; it is not to be found in bearing kids or in raising them. But women have been told for years by the Church and by Christian men that in pleasing men, and bearing and raising kids their satisfaction was to be found. But this only set women up for the feminist presentation, making it very hard for women to resist it. Feminism tells women that there must be something wrong with the system if they are unable to find satisfaction in it. This is what Satan hissed at Eve. "This lousy system of not being able to eat of this one tree is the problem as well as the One who gave you this silly system to begin with. I cannot believe God really told you not to eat of this perfectly good, desirable tree!" But the problem, of course, was not with the "system," but with the people in the system. But the feminists define the problem in God's system in two ways: in how it is ordered and in the nature of the woman.

Feminists believe that God ordered creation wrongly; that it should not be God, Christ, man, woman, but that man and woman are to be co-heads of creation. Although two-headed beings are seen as monstrous in all the rest of creation, this is what feminism believes humanity is to be. Therefore, feminism tells women that the reason why they cannot find satisfaction in this system is because it is ordered unfairly, and therefore, it oppresses them.

That women are unfairly oppressed is true, but the order of creation does not do this. The order is not the problem; the men and the women in the order are. Likewise, the Garden of Eden was not the problem, but Satan and the people in the garden were. But feminists tell women that their subordination or the patriarchy of men is the problem; if women could just break free of these, they would be satisfied. However, such a breaking away from the created order only leads to more dissatisfaction for women.

Consider this. The Greek word used in the Bible for submit is *hypotasso*. In military use of that time, it described an ordered army or fleet drawn up in battle array to function as a unit.[58] In a military order, rank says nothing about personal worth or even ability necessarily; it only describes the proper order for the military system. Although it may sound appealing, even the lowliest private would suffer if the order was abandoned, and women have suffered as God's order has been abandoned in His system. The order, "women and children first before men," is what protected women from brutal, aggressive men for centuries.

Even feminists seem to have a sense that we are dealing with something beyond merely societal convention. Something in this order touches deeply both men and women. Feminist Suzanne LaFollette wrote in 1926, "She [woman] was humble and subservient, as a matter of fact, for an incredibly long time; so long that there exists a general suspicion even at the present day that there is something in her nature which makes her want to be subject to man and to live as it were at secondhand."[59] And Virginia Woolf noted in 1918 that, "it is a perennial puzzle why no woman wrote a word of that extraordinary [Elizabethan] literature when every other man, it seemed, was capable of song or sonnet."[60] Also, one might note that there are no great female painters and no female Grand Master chess champions. But it goes the other way, too. There are few recorded superhuman feats of strength attributed to men. (In all cases that I have read about, a woman was involved.) And there are no recorded cases of a man giving birth.

To argue against such readily observable differences in men and women forces the feminists into illogical positions, and, therefore, towards things even more contrary to nature. For example, feminists have said (and most women today appear to believe it) that men rule because of the nature of the political and economic system. This is fallacious logic; it puts the cart before the horse, the chicken before the egg. The possible types of political and economic systems are limited by the nature of the human beings involved in them.[61]

Another favorite target of abuse by feminism is socialization: supposedly women submit to men because they are socialized to do so. But claiming socialization causes men to lead or women to submit is, "equivalent to one claiming that men more readily grow mustaches than women because little girls are told that facial hair is unfeminine."[62] God's order does not produce headship and sacrifice on the part of men and submission and surrender on the part of women, it merely reflects the reality He created in the individual parts of the system.

Feminism understands this, deep down, which is why modern feminism's prime attack has not been against the system or the order in the system—as it was in the nineteenth and early twentieth century—but against women themselves. The nature of woman which supports the order is what needs to be changed. While the early feminists sought to enhance and even magnify the nature of women, modern feminism has sought to deny or change it. Can anyone imagine Betty Friedan saying what Mary Wollstonecraft did in the eighteenth century? "As the care of children in their infancy is one of the grand duties annexed to the female character by nature, this duty would afford many forcible arguments for strengthening the female understanding, if it were properly considered."[63]

Today's feminists want to change women into beings of another kind by removing from them their natural inclination toward nurturing, compassion, and generosity.[64] This is the only way to make women more open to the feminist understanding of what is satisfying to women. And what better way to change the nature of women than abortion?

Of course, feminism did not start out advocating the

right of women to slaughter their babies; what woman, what christianized society, would have stood for that? So the program to fundamentally change the nature of women started with birth control. The 1910s feminist spoke in terms of controlling "their reproductive capacity free of state interference." Crystal Eastman, a feminist, said in 1918, "Birth control is an element essential in all aspects of feminism."[65] Miriam Allen de Ford said in 1976 of the 1920s era feminism that she personally experienced, "There were plenty of feminists and you knew who they were and they wrote individually or spoke individually, but there was no organized movement outside of birth control."[66]

It did not start with abortion, but it has ended there. The mother-child relationship is the most fundamental in all of nature, which is why humans react with repugnance to animals—and even insects and fish—which eat their young. Once the mother-child bond is broken, any and all social engineering is possible because the system itself is broken. If the system, society itself, does not see to its own propagation, it dies. Stagnant ponds and lakes die. Birth control effectively stagnates society because it regards new life coming into the system as suspect. But birth control is still a passive act against the system. Abortion is an active one. It is women tearing down their houses around them.

Around 1850 a book titled *The Science of Reproduction and Reproductive Control* made the assertion that birth control, limiting the number of children, put women "in a freer, a happier, and more independent position."[67] This is exactly what modern feminism came to say about abortion: women will be satisfied when they finally have the absolute right to their bodies as expressed by the right to kill their children. Of course, feminists are not satisfied even with abortion, but their fundamental nature as women is indeed changed. So is the entire divinely-ordained order and system that opposes abortion, and this is the real goal of feminism.

"God is not the author of confusion," says St. Paul. Satan is: he does not offer one competing religion but dozens, something for everyone. Sexual sin does not just come in one form but it degenerates into a dozen different perversions. Satan does not seem to care what lie or how many lies a person believes—only that he or she not believe the one truth. He offers a dozen lies; each one is designed to throw truth-seeking off track. Feminism is not one coherent, cohesive lie but a dozen different lies, half-truths, perversions, and twists designed to make the truth of God's male-female polarity unpalatable. Satan does not care what we believe about men, women, roles, and order as long as we do not believe the truth. So Satan has people right where he wants them when they are unsure, eclectic, or confused about the truth of God's created order. It is not that women believe the lie of feminism; it is that they do not know or believe the truth. This, too, leaves them perpetually unsatisfied.

This is how feminism leaves women: perpetually un-fulfilled, and therefore always empty and searching. It achieves this result by presenting a false dichotomy to women: they can either be women or they can be humans. The grand dame of feminism, Mary Wollstonecraft, advised women in the eighteenth century: "Willingly resign the privilege of rank and sex for the privilege of humanity."[68] Winifred Holtby recognized in 1926 that there are two strains of feminism—an old and a new: the new emphasized the importance of the women's point of view while the old emphasized their true humanity.[69] Writing in 1987, Nancy Cott continues to make out of the one woman two. She says women have always been and still are faced today with the challenge of "how to be human beings and women too."[70]

The truth of the matter is that women can only be human as women. "God made man in His own image, in the image of God He created him; male and female He created them" (Gn. 1:27). To deny one's gender is to deny one's humanity. Humanity does not exist apart from maleness and femaleness. This is true in more ways than one. Human beings do not come into existence apart from the joining of male and female, and they do not remain humans except by being either male or female. Jesus told us that in heaven we would be like the angels in the sense that we would neither marry nor be given in marriage, not in the sense that we would cease being males or females.

With feminism championing the false dichotomy between being female and being human, is it any wonder that women are confused, unsure of who they are and what they are suppose to be? Feminism perpetuates itself—makes it hard for women to resist it—by making two competing poles in women: female and human. The former can be only be satisfied with men, and the latter can only be satisfied without them or above them. Feminism dooms women to search for a satisfaction that cannot be found because it does not exist. A person cannot at one and the same time be satisfied with and without the very same thing.

Author Mary Kassian brings this all back to the fact that feminism denies women any rest in God. She comments in her book, *The Feminist Gospel*, "When feminists lost the God-imagery of masculinity and femininity taught in the Bible, they lost the ability to view themselves in the proper manner, and therefore lost the ability to interact properly with God."[71] This is another way of saying that their souls lost the ability to find their rest in God, and so as a result they truly are insatiable.

Feminism has always struggled against the gift of femininity that God gave to women. But the gifts of God are irrevocable; no matter what a woman does she is going to have to come to terms with this gift. An anti-suffragette said in 1909 that no matter how far astray women go mentally from the right appreciation of femininity, "sex will inexorably drive us back to wifehood and motherhood until the world ends."[72] A 1920s ex-feminist explained why she was an "ex" by saying that feminism had only superficially altered male and female roles. It left intact on the one side male egotism and on the other female maternal instinct. The latter prevented women from being as ruthless as men are in order to realize their individual ambitions and personal satisfactions.[73] Some gifts are just not alterable. We cannot take back the gift of water and ask that it not be wet, nor the gift of men and women and ask that they cease to be male and female.

The great authoress, Taylor Caldwell, although highly successful in a "man's world," did not deny her femininity; she did not "argue against her own juices." She was asked in 1977 if she felt satisfied now that her latest novel was so successful. She replied,

> There is no solid satisfaction in any career for a woman like myself. There is no home, no true freedom, no hope, no joy, no expectation for tomorrow, no contentment. I would rather cook a meal for a man and bring him his slippers and feel myself in the protection of his arms then have all the citations and awards and honors I have received worldwide, including the ribbon of the Legion of Honor and my property and my bank accounts.[74]

It is patently false to think that women can be genuinely satisfied as humans apart from their God-given femininity; even diehard feminists know this. Betty Friedan sounds strangely un-feminist and much like Caldwell when she writes of nineteenth century feminism that, "for the right to human growth, some women denied their own sex, the desire to have love and be loved by a man, and to bear children."[75] Again, we see her championing femaleness over against humanness in remarks she made to fellow feminist Simone de Beauvoir. She told Beauvoir that she believed women should have the right to stay home and raise children if they wanted to. Simon de Beauvoir's reply also shows how strong the pull of female polarity is: "No, we don't believe that any woman should have this choice. No woman should be authorized to stay at home to raise her children. Society should be totally different. Women should not have that choice, precisely because if there is such a choice, too many women will make that one."[76]

The female "pole" of humanity can only be matched and satisfied with the male "pole"; there is no generic "human pole." So when women, following the lead of feminists, set out to find this "human pole," they find it is impossible. But when they return to the male-female polarity in creation they find feminists, fellow women, barring the door. If they continue to pursue their femininity, they will be subjected to all manner of derogatory remarks. So women have no place for satisfaction.

The common explanation to the dissatisfaction of women is now genes or hormones or biology in some form. Science writer Maggie Scarf says, "Women are caught between the demands of their genes, urging them towards marriage and family, and a society sending them powerful new signals."[77] This view amplifies the author's contention that feminism leads women to "argue against their own juices." But other studies have shown that working women are just as depressed as those who stayed at home. This would suggest that mood is more a function of biology.

No matter which way we see the evidence we do not want to give in to a genetic, hormonal or biological understanding of feminine dissatisfaction. Giving in to a biological understanding of adolescence has given us unruly, undisciplined, and unsatisfied teenagers who are not called to repentance and quite frequently seek the solace of drugs to help them deal with their dissatisfaction. A biological understanding of the insatiability of women will not allow us to help them by calling them to repentance, and will leave them solace only in something that can rearrange their biology so they can be more satisfied, i.e., drugs. But the only help society (and, in many cases, the Church) offered women plagued by their disquietude has been drugs. (Legal drugs that alter chemicals in brains are prescribed much more for women than for men.) But drug-therapy for dissatisfaction is no help at all. The responsibility for their dissatisfaction must be laid—gently perhaps, but nevertheless firmly—on the hearts of fallen women. It must be laid on the hearts of fallen women who are ever-tempted to dissatisfaction and upon the shoulders of the feminist movement which constantly points women toward a satisfaction that does not exist and away from the only place satisfaction really is, in the God who gave them their femininity by making them female.

Notes:

[1] Friedan, The Feminine Mystique, (New York: Dell Publishing, 1983) 11.

[2] Degler, *At Odds*, (New York: Oxford University Press, 1980) 345.

[3] ibid., 354.

[4] Goldberg, *Why Men Rule*, (Chicago: Open Court, 1993) 229.

[5] Nicene and Post-Nicene Fathers, vol. 12, homily XXVI, 152.

[6] *The Feminist Papers*, ed. Alice S. Rossi, (Boston: Northeastern University Press, 1973) 672.

[7] G.K. Chesterton, *Orthodoxy*, (Wheaton: Harold Shaw Publishers, 1994) 166-167.

[8] Goldberg, 228.

[9] Will and Ariel Durant, *Rousseau and Revolution*, 219.

[10] The Feminist Papers, 102.

[11] *The Feminist Papers*, 103.

[12] Tocqueville, vol. 2, 214.

[13] Cott, *The Grounding of Feminism*, (New Haven: Yale University Press, 1987) 225.

[14] Goldberg, 33.

[15] Friedan, 242.

[16] Degler, 424ff.

[17] *The Feminist Papers*, 158.

[18] Goldberg, 116.

[19] Friedan, 211.

[20] Cott, 172, emphasis original.

[21] Douglas, *The Feminization of American Culture*, (New York: Alfred A. Knopf, 1977) 67.

[22] "Will the real feminists please stand?", *Current Thoughts and Trends*, April 1997, pp. 27-28.

[23] Friedan, 54.

[24] ibid., 72.

[25] ibid., 57.

[26] Cott, 172.

[27] ibid., 174.

[28] *The Feminist Papers*, 380.

[29] Friedan, 5.

[30] Carroll Quigley, *The World Since 1939: A History*, (New York: Collier Books, 1968) 597.

[31] Cott, 183-184.

[32] Degler, 448.

[33] Friedan, 311.

[34] Degler, 411.

[35] It is worth noting here that it was Marx and Engels who depicted women as household slaves oppressed by the bourgeois patriarchal family system. See *The Feminist Papers*, 123.

[36] Steichen, *Ungodly Rage*, (San Francisco: Ignatius Press, 1991) 264.

[37] Degler, 443.

[38] Cott, 180.

[39] Degler, 55.

[40] Friedan, 32.

[41] ibid., 122.

[42] ibid., 113.

[43] Gustave Flaubert, *Madame Bovary*, (New York: Penguin Books, 1964) 55.

[44] Thomas Hardy, *The Works of Thomas Hardy*, "The Return of the Native" (Stanford: Longmeadow Press, 1990) 561.

[45] Friedan, 381.

[46] Steichen, 379.

[47] Kassian, *The Feminist Gospel*, (Wheaton: Crossway Books, 1992) 40.

[48] ibid., 222.

[49] Friedan, 9.

[50] G.K. Chesterton, *What's Wrong with the World*, (San Francisco: Ignatius, 1994) 108.

[51] Vitz, *Psychology as Religion*, (Grand Rapids: Eerdmans, 1977) 121.

[52] Goldberg, 228.

[53] Elliot, *Let Me Be a Woman*, (Wheaton: Tyndale House Publishers, 1976) 75.

[54] ibid., 160.

[55] ibid., 75.

[56] Friedan, 17.

[57] ibid., 255.

[58] Clark, *Man and Woman in Christ*, (Ann Arbor: Servant Books, 1980) 81.

[59] *The Feminists Papers*, 542.

[60] ibid., 636.

[61] Goldberg, 143.

[62] ibid., 164 (emphasis original).

[63] *The Feminist Papers*, 72.

[64] Steichen, 94.

[65] Cott, 48.

[66] ibid., 282. (Cott says this statement reflects Ford's misconception, but I think Ford is accurate.)

[67] Degler, 202.

[68] *The Feminist Papers*, 78.

[69] Sommers, *Who Stole Feminism?*, (New York: Simon & Schuster, 1994) 19.

[70] Cott, 278.

[71] Kassian, 146.

[72] Degler, 352.

[73] Cott, 199.

[74] Horton, *Free to Stay at Home*, (Waco: Word Publishing, 1982) 27.

[75] Friedan, 81-82.

[76] Sommers, 256-257.

[77] Maggie Scarf, *Unfinished Business: Pressure Points in the Lives of Women*, (New York: Doubleday, 1980) 137.

www.ingramcontent.com/pod-product-compliance
Lightning Source LLC
Chambersburg PA
CBHW072012290326
41934CB00007BA/1070